Questions and Answers

SCHOOLS HISTORY PROJECT

Greg Lacey History Officer
Colin Shephard Chief Examiner

SERIES EDITOR: BOB McDUELL

Letts
EDUCATIONAL

Contents

HOW TO USE THIS BOOK	1
THE IMPORTANCE OF USING QUESTIONS FOR REVISION	2
ASSESSMENT OBJECTIVES IN HISTORY	2
SUMMARY OF ADVICE ON USING SOURCES	4
EXAMINATION TECHNIQUE	5

QUESTIONS AND REVISION SUMMARIES

1	A study in development: medicine through time	6
2	Depth study: Elizabethan England	12
3	Depth study: Britain, 1815–51	17
4	Depth study: the American West, 1840–95	21
5	Depth study: Germany, 1919–45	24
6	Paper 2	29
7	Mock examination paper	35

ANSWERS	39
Acknowledgements	78

Introduction

HOW TO USE THIS BOOK

The aim of the *Questions and Answers* series is to provide you with help to do as well as possible in your exams at GCSE level. This book is based on the idea that an experienced Examiner can give, through examination questions, sample answers and advice, the help students need to secure success and improve their grades.

This **Questions and Answers** series is designed to provide:

- Advice on the different types of question and how to answer them to maximise your marks.
- Information about the skills and types of understanding that will be tested on the examination papers. These are called the **Assessment Objectives**. The *Questions and Answers* series is intended to help you develop skills and understanding by showing you how marks are allocated.
- Many examples of **examination questions**, arranged by topic. Only try the questions once you have revised a topic thoroughly. It is best not to consult the answers before trying the questions.
- **Sample answers** to all the questions.
- **Advice from Examiners.** By using the experience of Chief Examiners we are able to give advice on how you can improve your answers and avoid the most common mistakes.

To use this book as effectively as possible it is important that you have information on the particular syllabus that you are studying. Each of the following Examining Groups has its own Schools History Project (SHP) syllabus:

- Midland Examining Group (MEG)
- Northern Examinations and Assessment Board (NEAB)
- Southern Examining Group (SEG)
- London Examinations

You need to know which of the above syllabuses you are studying, and which topics within the syllabus your teacher has chosen to cover. You will then know which sections of this book you should concentrate on. The examinations of all the Examining Groups are very similar. They consist of two written papers testing the **Development Study** (*Medicine Through Time* [MEG, NEAB, SEG, London]; Crime and Punishment Through Time [MEG, London]) and the **Depth Study** (*Elizabethan England* [MEG, NEAB, SEG]; *Britain, 1815-51* [MEG, NEAB, SEG, London]; *The American West* [MEG, NEAB, SEG, London]; *Germany, 1919-45* [MEG, NEAB, SEG, London]; South Africa, 1948-1995 [MEG]; Britain, 1900-1950 [London]).

This book includes examples of questions on all the Studies printed above in italics. The material is organised topic by topic, so that as you cover a topic in class, or in your revision, you can refer to the relevant section in this book, gaining valuable experience in practising your historical skills on real questions from previous examinations.

Even though some of the questions will not be taken from the syllabus you are studying, the material will still be of help to you, as the questions in the different Groups' examinations are of similar types, and the **Assessment Objectives** (that is, the knowledge, skills, and historical understanding being tested) are the same. Nonetheless, as good revision technique, you should also obtain copies of past papers for the syllabus you are studying, so that you are familiar with the content, style and layout of the particular papers and questions you will face in the examination.

History is not one of those subjects where, in general, the examiners are just looking for correct factual knowledge. They are concerned with how you use your knowledge to construct historical explanations. This book, then, is not intended to teach you the facts about the events you have studied – you can revise these from your class notes and textbooks. Instead, each section of this book will show you how to make the best use of what you already know, in order to do as well as you can in the examination.

Introduction

THE IMPORTANCE OF USING QUESTIONS FOR REVISION

Past examination questions play an important part in revising for examinations. However, don't start practising questions too early. Nothing can be more disheartening than trying to do a question which you do not understand because you have not mastered the topic. So study a topic thoroughly before attempting any questions on it.

How can past examination questions provide a way of preparing for the examination? It is unlikely that any question in this book will appear in exactly the same form on the papers you are going to take. However, the number of totally original questions that can be set on any part of the syllabus is very limited, so similar questions come up over and over again. It will help your confidence if the question you are trying to answer in the examination is familiar and you know you have done similar questions before.

Practising examination questions will highlight gaps in your knowledge and understanding, helping you to identify topics which you need to revise more thoroughly. It will indicate which sorts of questions you can do well. Attempting past questions will also get you used to the type of language used in examinations.

Finally, having access to sample answers, as you do in this book, will enable you to see clearly what the Examiner thinks is the best way of answering each question.

ASSESSMENT OBJECTIVES IN HISTORY

Assessment objectives are the qualities which are tested in the examination. There are three assessment objectives which are common to all GCSE History syllabuses. The wording of these objectives may vary slightly in the syllabuses of the different Examining Groups but don't worry about this; the objectives are essentially the same.

Objective 1: You should be able to recall, select, organise and deploy knowledge of the subject content.

This is the objective which is concerned with your factual knowledge of the topics you have studied, and your ability to organise and communicate that knowledge. In one sense, this is the most important objective of all, because without any factual knowledge you cannot demonstrate historical understanding, and without the ability to communicate you would never persuade the Examiner that you knew anything. Both of the other assessment objectives therefore depend on this one. However, on its own, this objective is not really what GCSE History is all about. Questions testing this objective alone would be concerned solely with the facts; no description, no argument, no analysis, no explanation. There will not be many of them, and they will require you simply to recall information about the events you have studied, but since factual knowledge is bound to be present in answers which relate to the other objectives, there is no real need to test it on its own. Objective 1 is an enabling objective – something which helps you to show your ability on the other objectives – rather than an end in itself. You need factual knowledge, and the more detailed and accurate your knowledge the better, but do not expect many questions which test Objective 1 alone.

Objective 2: You should be able to describe, analyse and explain a) events, changes and issues, and b) the key features and characteristics of the periods, societies and events that you have studied.

The importance of this objective is that it tests your ability to describe, analyse and construct explanations of historical events and developments. In GCSE History examinations you will not often be asked 'What happened…?'. Instead the questions might explore 'Why did it happen?', 'What did it change?', 'Why did people react to it in a certain way?'. These are not the kinds of

Introduction

questions to which answers will be correct or incorrect, because they involve opinions – *your* opinions. This does not mean that you can simply write down anything which occurs to you. For your opinions to have any value they must be supported by valid historical examples (which is where your knowledge of the events comes in).

Objective 2 questions will often involve certain concepts like continuity and change, or cause and consequence, around which historical explanations of events and issues are constructed. Questions in the examination may target one or other of these concepts to test the level of understanding you can demonstrate in your answer. Let's take the example of the development of antibiotics to show some of the different types of question which can test Objective 2.

- How was penicillin discovered? (description)
- Why was penicillin not developed before the 1940s? (explanation of causes)
- How important was the discovery of penicillin? (analysis of consequences)
- How far has the discovery of antibiotics changed the treatment of infection? (analysis of continuity/change)

In answering each of these questions you would have to describe, analyse and explain events. Later in this book you will find many examples of how to do this. Here it is enough to say that it matters much less what your explanation is, than how you go about constructing it. The Examiner has no single right answer in mind; what counts is the quality of thought that goes into your answer, and your ability to support thoughts with accurate and relevant historical examples.

An important aspect of analysing and explaining the key features and characteristics of societies you have studied is showing you understand the thoughts, motives and beliefs of people who lived in the past; that is, being able to view historical events from the perspective of people alive at the time. In explaining why something happened, it can often be relevant to include mention of the motives or beliefs of those involved in the events. In explaining why a development was important, its impact on the ways of life of the people affected by it can be significant. The Depth Study gives an excellent opportunity for the development of this kind of historical understanding.

Objective 3: In relation to the subject content you have studied, you should be able a) to comprehend, interpret, evaluate and use a range of sources of information of different types, and b) to comprehend, interpret and evaluate representations and interpretations of events, people and issues.

You will notice that this Objective has two elements, dealing first with sources and second with interpretations and representations. Sources are the 'raw materials' from which historians can find out about the past: documents, pictures, accounts, placenames, artefacts, and so on. Representations and interpretations are created when people try to reconstruct the past; this could be an historian writing about an event, a witness trying to remember what she had seen, or an artist drawing a picture of what a castle would have looked like hundreds of years ago. In practice, there is no clear dividing line between what counts as a source and what counts as an interpretation (in fact, most people would agree that all interpretations are themselves sources), and you certainly do not need to worry about the difference between them. In the examination you will be asked to deal with a range of sources of different types, and some of these will doubtless be interpretations. You can apply the same skills you have learnt during the course equally to sources and to interpretations.

Sources will be used in both your SHP examination papers, but in different ways. Watch out for 'stimulus material' questions. These include sources, but only to give you information to use in your answer. You are not required to interpret or evaluate the stimulus material. Such questions are used to test Objectives 1 and 2, but not Objective 3. If you aren't sure whether or not a question is targeting Objective 3, just ask yourself, 'Could I answer this question without using the source at all?' If the answer is 'Yes', then it is not an Objective 3 question.

However, most of the time when sources are included in the questions, the approach is very different. Here Objective 3 will be tested; that is, the questions will require you to interpret and

Introduction

evaluate the sources you are given. Questions on Objective 3 can be very varied in type. The following is a list of skills you might be expected to demonstrate:
- comprehension of sources;
- location and extraction of relevant information from the sources;
- distinguishing between fact and opinions;
- indicating deficiencies in sources, such as gaps and inconsistencies;
- detecting bias;
- comparing and contrasting sources;
- reaching conclusions based on the use of sources as evidence;
- comparing interpretations of an event;
- explaining how and why interpretations are created.

You will find examples of questions testing most of these in this book, along with detailed advice on how to answer them. But remember, when answering Objective 3 questions, never judge a source solely by its *type* – whether a photograph, a cartoon, an eye-witness account, a newspaper article etc. Always look at what the source actually tells you and consider its reliability in relation to your knowledge of the topic and the information you already have from other sources. The weakest answers to Objective 3 questions are always those which rely on generalisations, for example 'He was an eye-witness, so he must know what happened' or 'Primary sources are more reliable than secondary sources', and ignore what the source itself actually says or shows.

SUMMARY OF ADVICE ON USING SOURCES

The following five simple rules should help you to improve your answers to almost all source-based questions.

❶ Never be satisfied with judging the reliability or usefulness of a source by its type.

❷ Always use the content of a source in your answer.

❸ Do not take sources at face value. Look beneath the surface of the source to what you can infer from it – think about what the source really means, rather than just what it says.

❹ Do not automatically believe a source; always try to check what it says. An easy way to start checking is to ask whether any of the other sources you have says the same things. This is called cross-reference.

❺ Always use your knowledge of the topic to help you judge the reliability or usefulness of a source – in the light of what you know about the topic, can you believe the source or not?

Introduction

EXAMINATION TECHNIQUE

No book, however useful, will enable you to achieve a high grade if you have poor examination technique. In every examination you take, keep the following pieces of advice in mind:

❶ Read the questions carefully. Where there is a choice of questions, make sure you have read all the questions you could answer, and that you have chosen those you can answer best.

❷ Answer the right number of questions, and complete each question. Obey all the instructions, such as answering specific numbers of questions from different sections of the paper.

❸ Manage the time you have available effectively. Split the time sensibly between the questions you have to answer. There is little point in writing an enormous amount on a topic you know well, only to fail to complete your last question. All the marks available on questions you do not answer are marks lost to you, so finish the examination, even if it means cutting some answers shorter than you might wish.

❹ The question paper shows how many marks are available on each question. Use this as a guide to the amount of time to spend on each question. Do not write lengthy answers to questions which carry few marks.

❺ Answer the question as it is asked, and not how you might wish it to be. The most common fault in examination technique is irrelevance. Marks are only given for answers that do what the question asks.

❻ In History examinations you are expected to produce ideas, arguments, explanations. It is important to support these with relevant examples. Never make unsupported assertions.

❼ Remember that marks will be awarded for accurate spelling, punctuation and grammar. Check through your work carefully at the end of the examination and correct any errors.

1 A study in development: medicine through time

REVISION SUMMARY

This study focuses on the main changes in the history of medicine from prehistoric times to today. This may seem to be a lot to revise but do not worry, you will not be expected to have a detailed knowledge of the whole of the history of medicine.

1 You should have a basic knowledge of the main medical developments in the following periods

(a) Prehistoric times

(b) The ancient world – the Egyptians, Greeks and the Romans

(c) The Middle Ages

(d) The Medical Renaissance

(e) The nineteenth and twentieth centuries

2 You should know something about the different ideas people have had about the causes of disease, and the different treatments they have used

For example:

Ideas about cause	*Treatments*
Spirits and supernatural causes	Prayer, use of charms, trephinning
Channels in the body being blocked	Purging, blood letting
Theory of the Four Humours	Keeping the humours balanced by purging, blood letting, taking exercise, eating a balanced diet, clinical observation
Influence of the stars and planets	Studying star charts and using people's star signs for deciding which treatments were appropriate
Bad air and smells	Using flowers and herbs to cover the smells; keeping houses and streets clean
Spontaneous generation, germ theory	Use of antiseptics, antibiotics, vaccinations, public health systems

3 You should understand the following ideas about the history of medicine and be able to explain several examples of each idea

(a) Change in medicine happens at different speeds in different periods, e.g. slow change in the Middle Ages and rapid change in the nineteenth and twentieth centuries.

(b) Change sometimes brings benefits, sometimes disadvantages and sometimes both, e.g. the consequences of the use of the Theory of the Four Humours, the immediate and longer-term consequences of the use of anaesthetics in surgery.

A study in development: medicine through time

REVISION SUMMARY

(c) There have been periods of regression when medical knowledge and practice have gone into decline, e.g. the period of decline after the fall of the Roman Empire.

(d) Continuity – some medical ideas and practices have continued over long periods, e.g. the ideas of Galen, the Theory of the Four Humours and treatments such as blood letting.

(e) Old and new ideas often exist side by side, e.g. supernatural and natural explanations of disease in Ancient Greece.

4 You should be able to explain, by the use of precise examples, how a range of different factors have brought about or have hindered change in medicine

(a) Religion, e.g. medical knowledge gained from the embalming of bodies in Ancient Egypt, the banning of dissections of the human body by the Christian Church.

(b) War, e.g. Paré's discovery of an alternative to cauterisation, the mass production of penicillin during the Second World War.

(c) Government, e.g. the role of government in Rome in introducing a public health system, the role of government in introducing public health reforms in the nineteenth century and the National Health Service in Britain in the twentieth century.

(d) Science and technology, e.g. the part played by science in the study of germs in the nineteenth century, the part played by technology in the mass production of penicillin.

(e) Chance, e.g. Jenner's development of vaccination against smallpox, Fleming's discovery of penicillin.

(f) Individuals, e.g. Hippocrates, Galen, Paré, Vesalius, Harvey, Jenner, Lister, Simpson, Pasteur, Koch, Fleming.

It is important to remember that changes rarely happen because of just one of these factors, usually two or more are present combining to produce or hinder change. For example, if you look at the list you will notice that Paré's discovery of an alternative to cauterisation was helped by both war and chance. Be ready to explain other examples like this one.

QUESTIONS

1 Study Sources A–E and then answer questions (a)–(d) below.

SOURCE A

Order of King Edward III, written during the Plague in 1349.

> To the Lord Mayor of London.
> The human and other filth lying in the streets must be removed with all speed to places far distant.
> The King has learned how the city and suburbs are foul. There is so much filth from out of the houses by day and by night that the air is infected and the city poisoned to the danger of men... especially by the contagious sickness which increases daily.

1 A study in development: medicine through time

QUESTIONS

SOURCE B

From a Resolution passed by the Medical Men of Leeds in 1833.

> We are of the opinion that the streets in which cholera was most severe were those in which the drainage was most imperfect: and that the health of the inhabitants would be greatly improved by a general efficient system of drainage, sewerage and paving and better regulations for the cleaning of the streets.

SOURCE C

A diagram published by Dr Snow in 1854. It shows deaths from cholera in just 11 days in the area where people used the Broad Street pump for water.

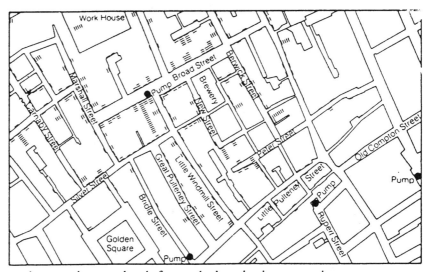

● – shows where a death from cholera had occurred

SOURCE D

Extracts from two articles about housing in Leeds, by James Hole, written in the 1860s.

> (i) from *'The Working Classes of Leeds'*, 1863
>
> The following table shows mortality in Leeds.
>
> | Year | Population | Deaths | Rate per 1000 |
> |------|-----------|--------|---------------|
> | 1855 | 109387 | 2640 | 24 |
> | 1862 | 111909 | 3484 | 29 |

The responsibility for this loss of life rests mainly on those who have the greatest power to remove it – the Corporation.
The Corporation can get powers to insist that all houses shall be connected with the new drainage. They could protect us against the wretched buildings that are run up by builders. The Corporation of Bradford have recently put a stop to new back-to-back dwellings, and their experience should be some encouragement to the Corporation of Leeds.

> (ii) from *'The Homes of the Working Classes'*, 1866

The Corporation and those who elect them are usually the owners of the property which needs improvement. Every pound they vote for drainage is something taken out of their own pocket.

A study in development: medicine through time

SOURCE E
Extracts from a government leaflet published in 1991.

> There has been a revolution in the nation's health over the last century. Better sanitation, improved diet and better health care have all contributed to an immense improvement. People today live longer, healthier lives. And we are still making progress... The National Health Service treats more patients than ever before.

(a) Study Sources A, B and C. Had public health services in towns in England improved by the middle of the nineteenth century? Use Sources A, B and C, and your own knowledge, to explain your answer. (5)

(b) Study Source D. Why were improvements in public health services slow? Use Source D, and your own knowledge, to explain your answer. (4)

(c) Study Sources D and E. In what ways do Sources D and E suggest that the pace of change in public health services was more rapid after the middle of the nineteenth century than in the 500 years before? (4)

(d) Why did public health services improve more rapidly after the middle of the nineteenth century? Use your own knowledge, to explain your answer. (7)

Edexcel specimen 1998

2 Study the following sources carefully and then answer the questions which follow.

SOURCE A
A cave painting from prehistoric times, found in Southern France. It is thought to show a medicine man.

1 A study in development: medicine through time

QUESTIONS

SOURCE B

From an Egyptian manuscript, written in about 1750 BC.

These are words to be spoken over the sick person. 'O Spirit, male or female, who lurks hidden in my flesh and in my limbs, get out of my flesh! Get out of my limbs!'

SOURCE C

From a book written by Hippocrates in about 4000 BC.

Man's body has blood, phlegm, yellow bile and black bile. These make up his parts and through them he feels illness or enjoys health.

SOURCE D

A drawing made in 1684 showing King Charles II touching for the 'King's Evil'.

(a) Study Source A. What does Source A suggest about prehistoric people's beliefs about the cause and cure of illness? (3)

(b) Read Source B and look at Source A again. Does Source B show that beliefs about the cause and cure of illness had made progress since prehistoric times (Source A)? Use your knowledge to help you to explain your answer. (5)

(c) Read Source C. What breakthrough did Hippocrates make in understanding about the cause and cure of illness? Use your knowledge as well as Sources A, B and C to help you to explain your answer. (7)

(d) Study Source D. Had there been no progress in understanding about the cause and cure of disease between the time of Hippocrates (Source C) and the time of Charles II (Source D)? Use your knowledge as well as the sources to help you to explain your answer. (10)

NEAB specimen 1998

A study in development: medicine through time

QUESTIONS

3 There is disagreement over the importance of Fleming's role in the discovery and development of penicillin.

   (a) Briefly describe Fleming's work. (5)

   (b) Explain why penicillin was not developed before the 1940s. (7)

   (c) 'The following were all equally important reasons why penicillin was developed:

      (i)   the work of Fleming;

      (ii) the work of Florey and Chain;

      (iii) chance;

      (iv) the Second World War.'

      Do you agree with this statement? Refer in your answer to (i), (ii), (iii) and (iv). (8)

      MEG specimen 1998

2 Depth study: Elizabethan England

REVISION SUMMARY

This study focuses on England during the reign of Elizabeth I. It is particularly important to understand the ideas, beliefs and attitudes of people of that time. Central themes are the personality of Elizabeth and how well she governed the country, the religious differences in Elizabethan England, Elizabethan attitudes towards the poor, the importance of the Elizabethan theatre and the achievements of Elizabethan seamen. The study provides an opportunity to develop an empathetic understanding of those ideas, beliefs and attitudes which unified the Elizabethans and an understanding of those which divided them. It also looks into questions like 'How well did Elizabeth deal with difficult problems such as Mary, Queen of Scots and the religious divisions in the country?', 'Who posed the greater threat to Elizabeth, the Puritans or the Catholics?' and 'Why was the theatre so popular during this period?'.

Depth study: Elizabethan England 2

1   Study the sources carefully, and then answer all the questions which follow.

SOURCE A
A scene at an Elizabethan theatre from a woodcut of the time.

2 Depth study: Elizabethan England

QUESTIONS

SOURCE B
An Elizabethan drawing of the Swan Theatre.

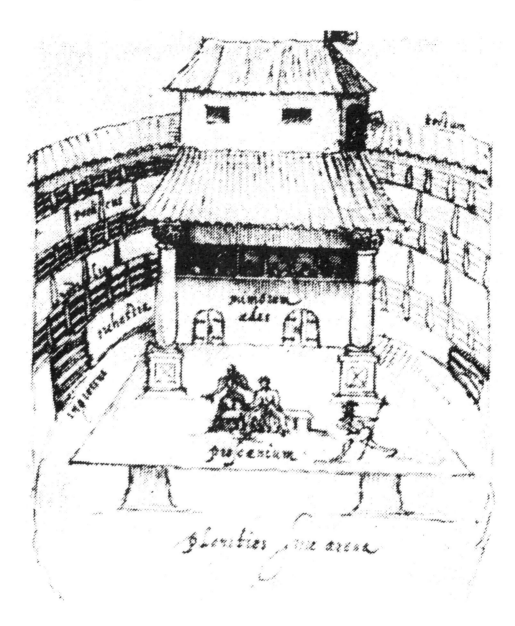

SOURCE C
From a petition by Lady Russell, Lord Hunsdon, and 29 other inhabitants of Blackfriars, London, to Elizabeth's Privy Council.

> Burbage has recently bought rooms near Lord Hunsdon's and is converting them into a common playhouse. This will be a great annoyance to the neighbourhood;
> (i) because of the gathering of vagrant and lewd persons on the pretence of coming to the plays,
> (ii) because it will make the place too crowded,
> (iii) in case of a return of sickness,
> (iv) because being near the church the drums and trumpets will disturb services.

Depth study: Elizabethan England

QUESTIONS

(a) Study Sources A, B and C. How far do these sources fully explain why theatres were popular in the Elizabethan period? (5)

(b) Study Source C.
Did problems such as those mentioned in this source make Elizabeth close all theatres? Use your knowledge of the period to explain your answer. (7)

(c) Study Source C. 'A member of the Common Council of London and a Puritan would not have reacted to this request in the same way.' Use your knowledge of the period to explain whether or not you agree with this statement. (8)

MEG specimen 1998

2 Study Source A and then answer all parts of Question 2.

SOURCE A

The execution of Mary, Queen of Scots in 1587: a drawing of the execution made at the time.

2 Depth study: Elizabethan England

QUESTIONS

(a) Source A is only a drawing. Does this mean that it cannot be trusted as evidence about the execution of Mary, Queen of Scots? Explain your answer. (5)

(b) What were the disadvantages in keeping Mary, Queen of Scots a prisoner? (6)

(c) Were the English Catholics a serious threat to Elizabeth? Support your answer with reasons and examples. (9)

(d) How important were Mary, Queen of Scots' own actions in bringing about her execution? Support your answer with reasons and examples. (10)

SQA specimen 1998

3 In the Elizabethan period there were many vagrants.

(a) Briefly describe the life led by vagrants in Elizabethan England. (5)

(b) In what ways were attitudes of the councils in towns such as Ipswich and Norwich towards the poor both different from and similar to the attitudes of the Elizabethan government? (7)

(c) 'The following were all equally important reasons for the large numbers of poor and unemployed in Elizabethan England:

  (i) agricultural enclosures;

  (ii) the rising population;

  (iii) rising prices;

  (iv) idleness.'

Do you agree with this statement? Refer in your answer to (i), (ii), (iii) and (iv). (8)

MEG specimen 1998

Depth study: Britain, 1815–51   3

REVISION SUMMARY

This study focuses on the conflicts between old and new in British society. It is particularly important to understand the ideas, beliefs and attitudes of different sections of society at that time, and the changes brought about by the Industrial Revolution and the impact of these changes. Central themes are the struggle to reform the electoral system, changing attitudes towards the poor, the living and working conditions of the poor in the industrial cities and in the countryside and attempts at reform, emigration from Britain, and the impact of the development of the railways. The study looks at questions like 'How effective was the 1832 Reform Act?', 'How were the poor affected by the introduction of the New Poor Law?', 'Why did people emigrate from Britain?' and 'Why did people disagree about the coming of the railways?'.

1 Prosperity and Poverty: Sources

QUESTIONS

SOURCE A

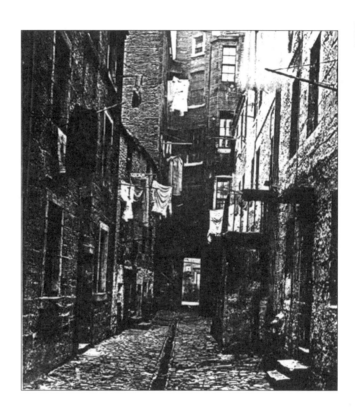

A photograph taken in Glasgow in the middle of the 19th Century.

SOURCE B

Shopping bought by a widow with four young children during a week in December 1839. This is from a survey of poor people in London published in 1841.

(s = shilling; d= old pence. There were 20 shillings in £1 and 12 pence in 1 shilling. One new penny (p) is worth about 2d.)

		s	d
Sunday:	Bought on Saturday night, Potatoes 1d., bacon 2d., candle 1d., tea and sugar 2d., soap 1d., coals 3d., loaf 8d.	1	6
Monday:	Tea and sugar 2d., butter 1d., candle 1d.		4
Tuesday:	Coals		2
Wednesday:	Tea and sugar 2d., candle 1/2d., wood 1/2., potatoes 1d.		4
Thursday:	Coals		1
Friday and **Saturday:**		0	0
		2s	5d

The woman pays 3s a week rent, owes £1 13s. Does cleaning and brushmaking; earned nothing this week; last week 3s; the week before 5s 8d. Might bring in £8 a year.

17

3 Depth study: Britain, 1815–51

QUESTIONS

SOURCE C

A description, written at the time, of the spending of a well-off family in 1824. Their yearly income is £1000.

> The family consists of a Gentleman, his Wife and three Children, they have three Female Servants, a Coachman and a Footman – in all ten persons. There is a four-wheeled carriage and a Pair of Horses. The household eats 52 lb of meat a week – 1lb for each person each day – in addition to fish and poultry. 1lb of butter each week is allowed and £1 1s a week is set aside for beer and other drinks. The smallest items are vegetables and fruit (9d each per week) and eggs and milk (4d each per week). The coachman receives £24 a year, the footman £22, the cook £16, the house-maid £14 14s, and the nursery-maid £10 10s. The two horses cost between them £65 17s a year.

SOURCE D

A drawing, made at the time, of a well-off family in the mid-19th century.

Depth study: Britain, 1815–51

SOURCE E

From a school text-book written in 1989. This extract deals with the effects of the Industrial Revolution in Britain during the first half of the 19th century.

> By 1851 more than half the people in Britain lived in towns which had over 50,000 people. The towns grew so fast that living conditions were terrible. The overcrowded, dirty conditions bred diseases. The worst of these was cholera. The Industrial Revolution increased the gap between rich and poor. Some people, like factory owners, made fortunes. In time, some of the skilled workers and mill hands also became better off. They enjoyed a much healthier diet. However, not all of the workers were doing well. The wages of some were rising but others lost their jobs altogether. Newly invented machines took jobs from skilled men who had previously earned good money. Those who could not find work often ended up in the workhouse.

SOURCE F

From a history of England written in 1872. This part of the book looks at the effects of the changes in Britain during the first half of the 19th century.

> The population, which more than doubled between 1760 and 1853, had a great improvement in comfortable living. People eat good white bread, and mountains of meat, poultry and game. For all of the 27,500,000 of the British population there is food enough and to spare. But amongst the growing prosperity there is hunger. Britain is fortunate in having her colonies, in which the most poverty-stricken can find a home and means of support. In this way the younger sons of our aristocracy who might have had to become tradesmen or even paupers, can find jobs in our Indian Empire to meet their needs. Even he who has eaten his last crust can find a ship that will take him, free of charge, to New Zealand or Australia, where, with a little work, he may live luxuriously every day.

SOURCE G

A drawing, made at the time, of people attacking the workhouse in Stockport, near Manchester, in 1841.

3 Depth study: Britain, 1815–51

QUESTIONS

1 (a) Study Sources A and B. How do Sources A and B help us to understand the problems of poverty in British towns in the middle of the 19th century? (5)

(b) Read Source C and study Source D. What are the main differences between the ways of life of the well-off families in Sources C and D, and the poor people in Sources A and B? (6)

(c) Which **TWO** of Sources A, B, C and D would you choose as the most reliable to show the differences between the lives of rich and poor in Britain in the first half of the 19th century? Use your knowledge of the period to help you to explain why you have chosen these sources. (8)

(d) Read Source E. Does Source E give enough evidence to explain why there was such a gap between the lives of the rich and the poor? Use Sources A, B, C, D and E and your knowledge of the period to help you to explain your answer. (9)

(e) Read Source F and read Source E again. Why do you think that Sources E and F give different interpretations of the effects of the changes in Britain during the first half of the 19th century? Use your knowledge of the period to help you to explain your answer. (10)

(f) Read Sources E and F again. Sources E and F mention two ways in which the problems of poverty were dealt with at the time. How useful do you find these sources to explain why people went to workhouses or emigrated? Use your knowledge of the period to help you to explain your answer. (10)

(g) Study Source G and read Source F again. Sources F and G suggest that emigration was more successful than the workhouses in dealing with the problems of poverty in Britain. Do you agree? Use your knowledge of the period to help you to explain your answer. (12)

NEAB specimen 1998

2 In 1832, after much discussion and several riots, the Reform Act was passed.

(a) Briefly describe the main criticisms of the electoral system before 1832. (5)

(b) How far was the electoral system improved by the 1832 Reform Act? Explain your answer. (7)

(c) 'The following were all equally important reasons why the Reform Act was passed in 1832:

(i) support for reform from the middle classes;

(ii) working-class riots, 1830–1832;

(iii) fear of revolution;

(iv) the activities of radicals such as Francis Place.'

Do you agree with this statement? Refer in your answer to (i), (ii), (iii) and (iv). (8)

MEG specimen 1998

Depth study: the American West, 1840–95   4

REVISION SUMMARY

This study focuses on the way in which the American West was settled during the period 1840–95. Central themes of the study are the relationships between white settlers and the Indians who already inhabited the Great Plains, and between the different groups of settlers. The study provides an opportunity to develop an empathetic understanding of the clash of cultures between the Indians and the groups of settlers who wished to take over the land, and of their different attitudes and lifestyles. It also looks into questions like 'Why did different groups of settlers move west?', 'How did the environment of the Great Plains affect the lives of people who settled there?' and 'Why were the Plains Indians unable to preserve their way of life?'.

QUESTIONS

1 Study the following sources:

   SOURCE A

   '*The Rocky Mountains, Emigrants Crossing the Plains*', a popular contemporary print.

4 Depth study: the American West, 1840–95

QUESTIONS

SOURCE B

Wagon Trails used by the settlers.

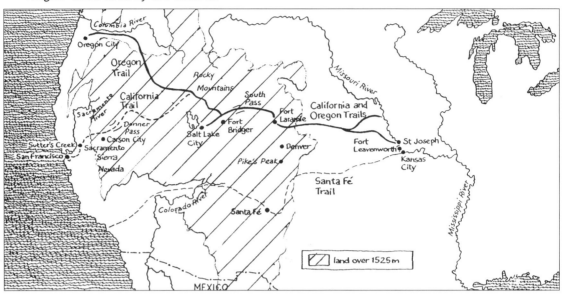

Now, using the sources and your own knowledge, answer the following questions:

(a) What were the dangers and difficulties of trail life? (6)

(b) Why were settlers willing to make such a hard and long journey? (7)

(c) Why was the far west settled before the Great Plains? (7)

SEG 1994

2 Study the following sources and answer the questions which follow.

SOURCE A

A picture called 'The First Season' showing homesteaders building a log cabin in 1874.

SOURCE B

A man writes a letter to *The Wichita Tribune* in the 1860s

In this town you may see young girls not over sixteen drinking whisky, smoking cigars, cursing and swearing until one almost loses the respect you should have for the weaker sex.

Depth study: the American West, 1840–95

SOURCE C

A female schoolteacher describes her interview for a job on the Great Plains in the 1860s

There was not the slightest sign of a toilet. I told the directors of the school that I could not teach if they did not build one. One of them said, 'Now you see what comes of hiring someone from outside. Never had any trouble before, plenty of trees to get behind.'

QUESTIONS

(a) Study Source A. What attitude do you think the person who drew Source A had to the role of women homesteaders on the Great Plains? (4)

(b) Read Sources B and C. Explain the different attitudes towards women on the Great Plains shown in Sources B and C. (6)

(c) Would women have welcomed their new lives on the Great Plains? Use **your own knowledge** and Sources A, B and C to help you to explain your answer. (10)

NEAB 1994

3 By 1890, with most Plains Indians living on reservations, the US government, and most white Americans, believed that they had solved what they called the 'Indian problem'.

(a) Briefly explain what the US government and white Americans meant when they talked about the 'Indian problem' in the West. (5)

(b) Explain why many Plains Indians found it difficult to live on the reservations. (7)

(c) Was the moving of the Plains Indians onto reservations the only reason why the white Americans were able to destroy the Indian way of life? Explain your answer. (8)

MEG 1997

5 Depth study: Germany, 1919–45

REVISION SUMMARY

This study focuses on events in inter-war Germany, looking at the causes of the rise to power of Hitler and the Nazi Party, and the impact of Nazi rule on different groups within the German population. In order to explain what occurred in the 1930s, it is necessary to look back into the period of the Weimar Republic, 1919–33, to see how developments at that time created a situation in which the Nazis could take power. The Depth Study allows the ideas, beliefs and motives of different people to be explored, and casts light on questions such as 'Why did the Germans allow Hitler to take power?', 'How successful was the Nazi Party in winning the support of the German people?' and 'Why did some Germans oppose the Nazis?'.

QUESTIONS

1 By the end of 1933 Adolf Hitler was the most powerful man in Germany.

   (a) Briefly describe Hitler's main political ideas. (5)

   (b) In what ways were the aims of the Weimar governments, 1919–33, both different from and similar to those of Hitler's government? (7)

   (c) 'The following were all equally important reasons for Hitler's powerful position by the end of 1933:

     (i) the Treaty of Versailles;

     (ii) the economic crisis of 1929–33;

     (iii) the personal qualities of Hitler;

     (iv) the Enabling Act of 1933.'

   Do you agree with this statement? Refer in your answer to (i), (ii), (iii) and (iv). (8)

MEG specimen 1998

2 Study the following sources and answer the questions which follow.

SOURCE A

A German cartoon from the 1930s about the SA.

Depth study: Germany, 1919–45

SOURCE B

Adolf Hitler writes to the leader of the SA in 1926

What we need is not 100 or 200 daring supporters but 100,000 or more fanatical fighters. We have to teach communism that National Socialism is the future master of the streets, just as it will some day be master of the state.

SOURCE C

In October 1933, Wilhelm Frick, Hitler's Minister of the Interior, writes to all SA leaders ordering them to control their men

Despite repeated announcements by the Chancellor, new offences and violence by leaders and members of the SA have been reported again and again during the past weeks. Above all, the SA have acted as police for which they have no authority. In future all police activities of the SA in all circumstances must cease.

(a) Study Source A. What do you think the person who drew Source A felt about the SA? (4)

(b) Read Sources B and C. Sources B and C show different attitudes towards the activities of the SA. Why do you think this is so? (6)

(c) Germans at this time had different views about the SA. Why was this so?
Use **your own knowledge** and Sources A, B and C to help you to explain your answer. (8)

NEAB 1995

3 Study the following sources carefully, and then answer all the questions which follow.

SOURCE A

A photograph of the racial examination of a young girl in Nazi Germany.

5 Depth study: Germany, 1919–45

QUESTIONS

SOURCE B

A cartoon published in a German magazine in March 1932.

'Father, why must we freeze at home when there is so much coal?'

'Because the hand of the Jew lies heavily on the people.'

Depth study: Germany, 1919–45

SOURCE C

This chart produced by the Nazis shows how over 120 years the population of Germany will become corrupted if there are too many 'criminal families' and not enough 'valuable families'. The 'valuable families' are those at the top in white.

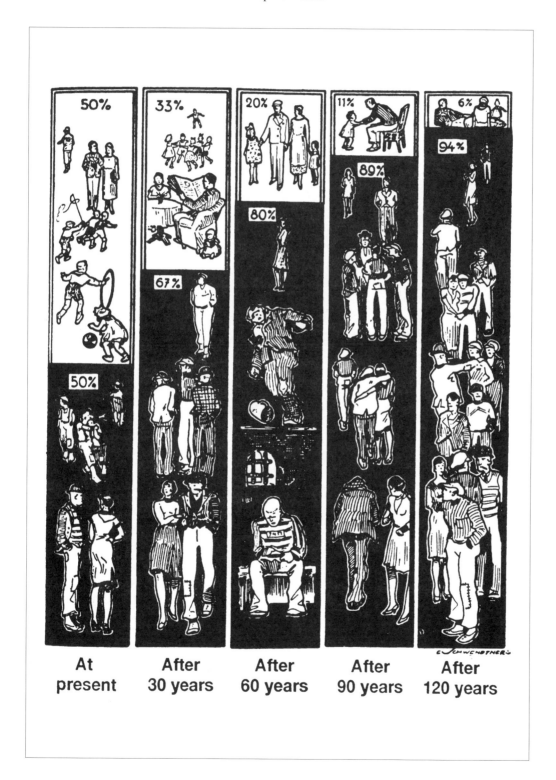

5 Depth study: Germany, 1919–45

QUESTIONS

(a) Study Source A.

Use your own knowledge to explain why the Nazis carried out 'racial examinations' of people in Germany. (7)

(b) Study Source B.

Was Hitler's hatred of the Jews the main reason why they were persecuted in Nazi Germany? Use your own knowledge to explain your answer. (6)

(c) Study Source C.

Not only Jews were persecuted in Nazi Germany. Use your own knowledge to explain why other groups of people were persecuted by the Nazis. (7)

MEG 1997

Paper 2 — 6

SOURCES EXERCISE ON THE DEVELOPMENT STUDY

REVISION SUMMARY

The London, MEG and SEG examinations all include in Paper 2 a compulsory extended sources exercise set in the context of the Development Study. For London and MEG, this exercise is the whole paper, and for SEG it is more than half. Each year it is set on a different topic, which is notified to teachers in advance, so you will know which section of the syllabus to revise for it.

The exercise is designed to test your ability to use a collection of different types of historical source. You will be given a set of sources on the nominated issue or problem. There will also be a number of questions to answer. You will be expected to use your knowledge of the topic to help you interpret and evaluate the sources; many of the questions will actually instruct you to 'use the sources and your own knowledge'. This is to remind you that the judgements you reach about the sources need to make sense in the light of what you know about the topic.

All the questions are compulsory, so make absolutely sure that you answer them all. However, do not rush to start writing. It is important that you read the background information and the sources carefully before you try to answer any of the questions. If not, you may find that you miss important information, or fail to spot opportunities to cross-reference – testing what one source says against a different account in another source.

Incidentally, you will be given some details on the provenance of each source – for instance, who wrote it, when it was written and the circumstances in which it was written. You must accept these details as true. Some students told, for example, that Source A is a photograph taken of a heart operation in Cape Town in 1968, have taken to questioning the provenance, and suggesting, say, that it could equally well be a photograph of a kidney transplant operation in London in 1985. This earns no marks whatsoever. The details on provenance given to you will be accurate – if they were open to doubt, every source could be rejected as not being what it claimed.

The questions will generally be arranged to work through all the sources, one or two at a time. This will help you to look carefully at each source in turn, and get to grips with what exactly it says. In answering a question you must use the source or sources to which you are specifically referred, but there is nothing to prevent you also using other sources in your answer if they are relevant. At the end, there will be one or two questions which require you to use all the evidence. By the time you get to these questions, you will have already answered earlier questions on each of the sources. In answering these last questions do not forget the judgements you have already made on individual sources earlier in the exercise. It is surprising how often in these questions students will accept sources as reliable which they have earlier dismissed as useless.

The kinds of questions used in the Paper 2 sources exercise are very varied, but they are all designed to test your ability to comprehend, interpret and evaluate the sources you have been given, using your knowledge of the topic.

The management of time on this exercise is very important. You have a set of sources to read and comprehend, and then several questions to answer. Take notice of how many marks are available on each question, and do not write too much on questions carrying small numbers of marks. It is a very common mistake for students to write far too much on the first couple of questions, and then find themselves very short of time at the end.

Finally, the main weakness of answers in this exercise is a willingness of candidates to restrict their answers to generalisations about source type or about the author of the source, rather than using the content of the source, and their knowledge of the topic. There are two particular problem areas: the issue of bias, and the labelling of sources as primary or secondary.

Bias – for many students, the idea of bias means simply that you cannot ever believe anything in any source. For these students, all sources are bound to be biased, and therefore of no use whatsoever to historians. If this were the case, writing history would be even more of a problem

REVISION SUMMARY

than it actually is; but, of course, it is not the case. Anyone, in constructing an account, may have reasons for wanting to present the account in a certain way, perhaps, say, by leaving out some embarrassing material. There is a huge variety of possible motives for shaping an account in a particular way, but the fact that this happens does not necessarily make the account useless or unreliable. Indeed, people are bound to have different opinions and viewpoints about an event, and finding out about these is just as important for an historian as finding out about the events themselves. So bias is actually a help to historians in finding out about how people viewed the past. If you find yourself tempted to write that a source is useless because it is biased, think again. Think what you can do with the source *because* it is biased.

Primary/secondary – these words are labels that people give to sources. They cause more trouble to students answering sources questions than any other two words. Unfortunately, many students seem to have the idea that primary/secondary means better/worse, as in 'Primary evidence is bound to be better than secondary because it is produced by people who were actually there and they would know what happened.' Or alternatively it might mean worse/better as in 'Secondary evidence is bound to be more reliable because the writer has had time to study the events and work out what really happened, but those there at the time only saw a small part of the event.' Please resist the temptation to write generalisations like these – they will only earn low marks. Judge each source on its own merits – not on whether you think it is primary or secondary, but on the basis of what the source actually says or shows.

QUESTIONS

Study the Background Information and the sources carefully, and then answer **all** the questions which follow.

WHY DID FLEMING GET ALL THE CREDIT FOR PENICILLIN?

Background Information

In the late nineteenth and early twentieth century much progress was made in developing new drugs to fight infections, but the new drugs were powerless against some germs. In 1928 Alexander Fleming discovered the penicillin mould. This destroyed most germs but did not harm healthy tissue. However, only a very small part of the mould was pure penicillin, and Fleming found it difficult to produce this pure penicillin. It was also not known whether penicillin would work on humans.

Ten years later, after reading about Fleming's work, two scientists at Oxford, Howard Florey and Ernst Chain, began to investigate penicillin. They found a way to produce small amounts of pure penicillin. In 1940 they tested the drug on infected mice and it worked. They then tested it on humans and it cured patients who would have normally died of their infections. In 1942 Fleming asked Florey for some penicillin for a patient who was dying. The patient completely recovered. The newspapers got hold of the story and called penicillin 'the miracle cure'. In all the publicity that followed it was Fleming who was given all the credit. Why was this?

SOURCE A

An extract from Howard Florey's account of the discovery of penicillin written in 1944.

In 1928 Fleming was studying the staphylococcus germ in his laboratory in St Mary's Hospital in London. One day he put to one side on his bench a plate on which staphyloccus germs were growing. Several days later there was mould growing on one side of the plate. Fleming noticed that near the mould the germs were disappearing. He grew the mould and used experiments to show it stopped the growth of many bacteria which caused disease in human beings. However, when he tried to extract the pure penicillin from the mould he failed. He reached the conclusion that penicillin was unlikely to have any practical value in medicine.

SOURCE B

An account of the discovery of penicillin from a book on the history of medicine published in 1987.

In 1928 Fleming was studying the staphylococcus germ in his laboratory in St Mary's Hospital. He had dozens of glass dishes stood in a bowl of disinfectant ready for cleaning. Some of the dishes were still above the level of the disinfectant. Fleming picked up one of the dishes and it was then he made his great discovery. Mould was growing on the dish and no germs were growing near the mould. 'That's funny!' he said, and picked off a tiny piece of mould and put it carefully in a dish of jelly where it could grow. Fleming found that the mould killed the germs that caused diphtheria, gangrene and meningitis. Fleming worked hard for a time on the mould. He tried to purify the mould juice but this needed skills in chemistry that were not available at the time. He wrote articles describing the work and calling the substance 'penicillin', but then he returned to his routine work. He kept a supply of the mould but he did no more to develop it.

SOURCE C

A photograph of Fleming in his laboratory in 1928.

6 Paper 2

QUESTIONS

SOURCE D

From a biography of Fleming published in 1984.

The newspaper campaign between 1942 and 1945 made Fleming one of the most famous men in the world. It might be claimed that this was only to be expected, since penicillin was a tremendous discovery and Fleming the discoverer. But, in 1942 when the campaign began, penicillin had been used in a very few cases and was available only in Oxford. Florey, in his letters, writes bitterly of a dishonest campaign designed to give Fleming and St Mary's Hospital all the credit for the work done in Oxford. He seems to blame Fleming for being interviewed and photographed, and for claiming that the Oxford work had merely confirmed his own researches.

SOURCE E

From a book about Fleming published in 1985.

Reporters descended on Oxford but Florey refused to see them. Not surprisingly, the reporters resented this since they needed a good story. They went back to London and a warmer welcome at St Mary's which was near financial collapse and needed publicity to bring in funds. Sir Almoth Wright, Fleming's head of department, had throughout his career used the press to his own advantage. Publicity for penicillin would improve the reputation of the hospital and his department.

SOURCE F

From a letter published in The Times newspaper, 31 August 1942, from Sir Almoth Wright, head of the department in which Fleming worked at St Mary's Hospital.

In the leading article on penicillin yesterday you failed to give anyone the credit for this discovery. I would point out that it should be given to Professor Alexander Fleming of this research laboratory. For he is the discoverer of penicillin and was the person who first suggested that penicillin might prove to have an important use in medicine.

SOURCE G

From an American magazine published on 15 May 1944.

The man who made this great reduction in human suffering is Alexander Fleming discoverer of the mould from which penicillin is made. He is a short, shy Scot with dreamy blue eyes, fierce white hair and a lightning-quick mind. It will be hard to say who the great men of the 20th century are but Fleming is certainly one of them.

SOURCE H

From a letter from Florey to the President of the Royal Society (an organisation of important scientists), 11 December 1942.

As you know, there has been a lot of undesirable publicity in the newspapers about penicillin. I have taken a firm line and said that there was to be no interviews with the press. I have had a letter from Fleming in which he assures me that he was trying to do the same. I now have evidence from the BBC, and also from some people at St Mary's, that Fleming is trying to do his best to see that the whole subject is presented as having been worked out by Fleming.

SOURCE I

From a letter from Fleming to Florey, 2 September 1942.

Although my work started you off on the penicillin hunt, it was you who have made it a practical proposition, and it is good that you should get the credit. You are lucky in Oxford to be out of the range of reporters.

SOURCE J

From a speech by Fleming to American scientists, 13 December 1943.

Nothing is more certain than when in September 1928 I saw bacteria fading away next to the mould, I had no suspicion that I had got a clue to the most powerful substance yet used to defeat bacterial infection of the human body.

6 Paper 2

QUESTIONS Study the Background Information and the sources carefully, and then answer **all** the questions which follow. In answering the questions you are expected to use your knowledge of the topic to help you interpret and evaluate the sources and to explain your answers. When you are instructed to use a source you must do so, but you may also use any of the other sources which are relevant.

1. Study Sources A and B.
   How far do these sources agree about the discovery and development of penicillin?
   Explain your answer. (5)

2. Study Source C.
   How useful is this source as evidence about the discovery and development of penicillin?
   Explain your answer. (5)

3. Study Sources D and E.
   Does Source E support the claims made in Source D?
   Explain your answer. (6)

4. Study Sources F and G.
   Which one of these two sources is the more reliable?
   Explain your answer. (7)

5. Study Sources H, I and J.
   Do Sources I and J prove Source H to be wrong?
   Explain your answer. (7)

6. Study all the sources.
   How far is the following statement supported by the sources in this paper?
   'Fleming deliberately grabbed the glory for the development of penicillin.'
   Use the sources and your knowledge to explain your answer. (10)

Mock examination paper 7

FLORENCE NIGHTINGALE AND MARY SEACOLE IN THE CRIMEA

REVISION SUMMARY

Background Information

The Crimean War took place from 1854 to 1856. Britain, France and Turkey fought against Russia mainly in the area called the Crimea.

According to official government reports the war was being conducted efficiently. But reports from journalists of 'The Times' told another story. Their reports about the dreadful conditions and lack of care of the wounded soldiers caused a scandal in Britain.

This paper concentrates on the work of two women who went out to the Crimea to look after the wounded soldiers. One was Florence Nightingale. She had been very successful as superintendent of a hospital in London and was invited by the British government to go to the Crimea. She left in October 1854 taking thirty-eight nurses with her. The other was Mary Seacole. Mary was from Jamaica, where without any formal training, she had practised as a doctor and earned the respect of many British soldiers stationed there. She paid her own way to London and volunteered to go to the Crimea with Florence's nurses. But she was turned down. She then made the three week journey to the Crimea at her own expense.

Both women made important contributions to the welfare of the soldiers in the Crimea. But did they contribute in similar or different ways?

*Try to complete this paper in one sitting of **one hour**.*

QUESTIONS

SOURCE A

Written by a historian in 1984 in introduction to a new edition of Mary Seacole's autobiography 'Wonderful Adventures of Mrs Seacole in many lands', which was first published in 1857

How different were the skills and experience which Mary Seacole and Florence Nightingale brought to the suffering army. At the hospital in Scutari Florence's role was administrative. Regulations and tradition prevented her nurses from performing any but the most basic duties. They were involved in undoing bandages, washing wounds before inspection by the medical officer and spoon-feeding the patients on special diets. They were rarely seen outside the wards. As for Mary, as soon as she arrived, even before she had established her hotel, she threw herself into the work of relieving the suffering among the troops. There were times when she refused to wait for the cease-fire and picked her way through the mutilated bodies of men, looking for the wounded.

SOURCE B

Dr John Hall, Chief of Medical Staff of the army in the Crimea, writing in October 1854 to Dr Andrew Smith, the Director General of the Army Medical Service. Hall believed in strict discipline and did not want the troops to be 'pampered'.

I have much satisfaction in being able to inform you that the whole hospital establishment in Scutari is now in a highly satisfactory state and that nothing is lacking.

7 Mock examination paper

QUESTIONS

SOURCE C

A description of the conditions in the hospital at Scutari from a letter from Florence Nightingale to a member of the British government in November 1854 shortly after Florence's arrival in the Crimea.

It appears that in these hospitals the Purveyors consider washing both of linen and of the men as an unimportant 'detail'. During the three weeks we have been here no washing has been performed for the men either of body-linen or of bed linen except by ourselves and a few wives of the wounded.

When we came here there was neither basin, towel nor soap in the wards, nor any means of personal cleanliness for the wounded.

(The Purveyors were responsible for ordering supplies for the army.)

SOURCE D

A contemporary drawing of one of the wards in the hospital in Scutari in 1856

SOURCE E

From a book about the history of medicine published in 1997.

On 4 November 1854 Nightingale and her nurses arrived at Scutari, where nearly two thousand wounded and sick lay in the foul rat-infested wards. She immediately ordered three hundred scrubbing brushes. The hospital was soon full of the wounded. Nightingale organised the nursing of the sick. She provided meals, supplied bedding, and saw to the laundry. (She said about herself 'I am a kind of General Dealer in socks, shirts, knives and forks, wooden spoons, tin baths, tables, cabbages and carrots, operating tables, towels and soap.') Within six months she had transformed the place, slashing the death rate from about 40 per cent to 2 per cent.

Mock examination paper 7

SOURCE F

From a book about the Crimean War, published in 1997.

There were many complaints about the British orderlies who were often drunk and stole from the wounded soldiers. Nevertheless, Florence Nightingale thought that male orderlies and not nurses should be tending the sick. Meanwhile, the female nurses performed domestic chores and gave the patients 'womanly attentions'.

Nightingale did not think it proper for female nurses to come into close contact with male patients. She did not allow her nurses in the wards after 8.30 pm, and she thought it was only acceptable for certain parts of the men's bodies to be washed by the nurses. One of her nurses, Elizabeth Davies, wanted a more practical role. The only way of doing this was to leave Scutari against Nightingale's wishes and go nearer to the front.

SOURCE G

From Mary Seacole's autobiography published in 1857. Her autobiography was called 'Wonderful Adventures of Mrs Seacole in many lands'.

On my very first day, a party of sick and wounded had just arrived. Here was work for me, I felt sure. With so many patients, the doctors must be glad of all the hands they could get. Indeed, so strong was the old impulse within me, that I waited for no permission, but seeing a poor artilleryman stretched upon a pallet, groaning heavily, I ran up to him at once, and eased the stiff dressings. Lightly my practised fingers ran over the familiar work, and well was I rewarded when the poor fellow's groans turned into a restless, uneasy mutter. God help him! He had been hit in the forehead, and I think his sight was gone. I stooped down, and raised some tea to his baked lips. Then his hand touched mine and rested there.

SOURCE H

(i) An army surgeon writing in 1855 to his family in England.

Here I met Mrs Seacole, who out of the goodness of her heart and at her own expense, supplied hot tea to the poor sufferers. In rain and snow she was at her self-chosen post with her stove and kettle, in any shelter she could find, brewing tea for all who wanted it.

(ii) From a report by a journalist of 'The Times' newspaper.

Her hut was surrounded every morning by the rough navvies and Land Transport men, who had a faith in her skills in healing, which she justified by many cures and by removing obstinate cases of diarrhoea, dysentery, and similar complaints.

7 Mock examination paper

QUESTIONS

Study the Background Information and the sources carefully, and then answer **all** the questions which follow.
In answering the questions you are expected to use your knowledge of the topic to help you interpret and evaluate the sources and to explain your answers. When you are instructed to use a source you must do so, but you may also use any of the other sources which are relevant.

1. Study Source A.
   According to this source were the contributions of Florence Nightingale and Mary Seacole similar or different? Explain your answer. (4)

2. Study Sources B and C.
   These two descriptions of conditions in Scutari hospital are very different.
   Does this mean that one of them must be wrong? Explain your answer. (7)

3. Study Sources D and E.
   Which one of these two sources is more useful? Explain your answer. (6)

4. Study Sources F and G.
   How far do these two sources give similar impressions of Florence Nightingale and Mary Seacole? Explain your answer. (5)

5. Study Sources G and H.
   Do you believe both of these sources? Explain your answer. (8)

6. Study all the sources.
   How far do these sources support the view that Florence Nightingale and Mary Seacole made important, but very different, contributions to the nursing of the soldiers in the Crimea. Make sure you use your own knowledge to interpret and evaluate the sources. (10)

Answers

1 A STUDY IN DEVELOPMENT: MEDICINE THROUGH TIME

Answer — **Mark**

1 (a) Study Sources A, B and C. Had public health services in towns in England improved by the middle of the nineteenth century? Use Sources A, B, and C, and your own knowledge, to explain your answer. **(5)**

> **Examiner's tip** Remember to use your knowledge of the development of public health and not to depend just on what the sources say. Answers restricted to what is in the sources will be awarded no more than 1 mark! These three sources suggest that public health services had not improved much by the middle of the nineteenth century with people dying from cholera in Source C after drinking polluted water. You could add to this from your own knowledge by explaining what improvements were attempted by the middle of the century, e.g. those made possible by the 1848 Public Health Act. You could also explain that the growth of large industrial towns made the problems of public health much greater. Be careful not to write about developments later in the nineteenth century like the 1875 Public Health Act. This question is asking you about improvements that had taken place by the middle of the century. The first answer which follows is based just on the sources and would receive 1 mark. The second answer would have scored full marks because the candidate has used her knowledge of the period to add to the sources.

Answer 1 Public health services were still bad. Source B shows that there were no proper drains and Source C shows lots of people dying from cholera. This tells me that public health had not been improved much.

Answer 2 Public health services had improved a little by the middle of the nineteenth century but Sources B and C show that much still had to be done. In 1848 a Public Health Act was passed. This allowed local councils to improve public health facilities in their own area and to borrow money to pay for the improvements. However, not many councils bothered to do this but some towns did begin building sewers and providing clean water supplies especially after bad outbreaks of cholera. Of course the problem of public health was made even worse by the growth of large towns like Leeds where people were crammed into small houses and where the lack of sewers and clean water was even more of a problem. Rubbish collected in the streets and water supplies quickly became polluted. Disease spread more easily and this was why there were so many outbreaks of cholera.

(b) Study Source D. Why were improvements in public health services slow? Use Source D, and your own knowledge, to explain your answer. **(4)**

> **Examiner's tip** This question is asking you to explain why improvements were slow. You must explain some reasons and not just describe the state of public health. Source D suggests two reasons which you should explain more fully. First, it says that the Corporation (the Council) of Leeds had not bothered to request the powers it needed to make sure that all houses had drains. You could develop this by explaining that the 1848 Public Health Act made it possible for local councils to request these powers from the Board of Health but that as it was not compulsory many did not bother because they did not like interference from central government.
> Secondly, the last part of Source D mentions that the voters do not want to pay for the improvements. This could be developed by explaining that the middle classes did not live in the worst parts of the towns and did not see why

Answers to Unit 1

Answer	Mark

> they should pay higher rates to improve living conditions for the poor. Many believed that people should look after themselves and not depend on others. You could add some other reasons of your own. For example, you could explain that the connection between germs and disease was not yet proved and so people could see little point in improving public health. But be careful not to write too much as there are only four marks for this question. Briefly explain a couple of reasons and then move on.
> The first answer given below would be given one mark only as it simply states one of the points in the source. It does not explain the point. The second answer explains two reasons and would be awarded full marks.

Answer 1 Improvements were slow because they cost a lot of money and nobody wanted to pay for them.

Answer 2 Improvements were slow because the Public Health Act failed to force local councils to do anything about Public Health. It gave them the powers if they wanted to but Source D shows that the Leeds Corporation did not bother. Most Corporations were like the one in Leeds and did nothing. If the government really wanted something to be done they should have made the improvement of public health compulsory. Also Pasteur was only just beginning to develop the germ theory. While people did not know that germs caused diseases like cholera they would not bother to provide clean water and clean living conditions for everyone.

(c) **Study Sources D and E. In what ways do Sources D and E suggest that the pace of change in public health services was more rapid after the middle of the nineteenth century than in the 500 years before?** (4)

> **Examiner's tip** Remember not simply to copy out the changes in Source E. This will only get you one mark. Start with the changes in Source E but then use your knowledge to show how change has been much quicker since 1850 than in the previous 500 years. The question does ask about 'the pace of change' so you must show how the pace has got quicker rather than just mention some changes. The answer given below does this.

Since 1850 public health had changed very quickly. Proper drains, sewers and fresh water are now provided for everyone. Lots of new houses have been built which are not crowded and damp and are much healthier to live in. The National Health Service provides free health care for everyone. Before, many people could not afford to go to the doctor or to hospital. The government has introduced lots of vaccinations for all children and these protect them from disease. All of this has been done in the last 150 years and the death rate has fallen with people living much longer. In the 500 hundred years before the nineteenth century there was little change. Rubbish collected in the streets, people used polluted water, there were few proper doctors and people could not afford them and the death rate was high. Nothing changed for hundreds of years.

(d) **Why did public health services improve more rapidly after the middle of the nineteenth century? Use your own knowledge to explain your answer.** (7)

Answers to Unit 1

Answer	Mark

> **Examiner's tip** You will have noticed that this question carries more marks than the other questions. This does not necessarily mean that you have to write more, but it does mean that you have to explain reasons rather than just describe. You must try and explain how at least two reasons helped bring about rapid improvements. Make sure you do not just mention the reasons without explaining how they brought about change. It is better to explain one reason properly than to list five or six reasons without explaining any of them! Make sure you use specific examples to back up your answer.
> Reasons for the rapid improvement in public health could include: the germ theory, more people able to vote, improvements in technology, the Second World War. Remember – explain how at least two of these helped to bring about improvements. The answers given below would get very different marks. The first answer gives some good reasons but fails to explain how they helped bring about improvements. The second answer explains several reasons and even shows how these reasons acted together to bring about improvements. This is always a good way of achieving high marks.

Answer 1 There was rapid improvement because governments were more willing to improve conditions and because people knew that germs caused disease. Improved technology also meant that they could build better drains and sewers than ever before.

Answer 2 One of the reasons why there was a lot of improvement was that Pasteur and Koch showed that germs cause disease. People now knew that diseases like typhus and tuberculosis were caused by living in damp dirty conditions. This was helped by John Snow who showed how cholera was caused by dirty water. All this convinced the government and town councils that something had to be done. They could now see a reason for building proper drains and sewers and providing clean water. Another reason why the government acted was because in the 1860s ordinary working-class people were given the vote. To win their support politicians had to look after them by providing better public health. So all these reasons came together at roughly the same time to force the government to do something. As a result the government passed the 1875 Public Health Act which forced town councils to provide public health facilities. Once laissez-faire attitudes had been defeated later governments would pass more and more reforms.

---

2 (a) Study Source A. What does Source A suggest about prehistoric people's beliefs about the cause and cure of illness? (3)

> **Examiner's tip** There are two important points to make in your answer. First: the figure in Source A is thought to show a medicine man. This tells you that people at that time believed spirits or gods caused and cured illnesses. Second: you are told that the figure only *might* be a medicine man. So it is worth making the point that because of this the source is not definite evidence about people's beliefs about the cause and cure of illness. The answer below makes both these points and would gain all three marks. If you were to make just one of these points you would score two marks.

I am not sure if Source A tells me anything because it is not definite that it is a medicine man. It could be nothing to do with medicine. However, if it is a medicine man

Answers to Unit 1

Answer | Mark

then it tells me that people at that time believed that illness was caused and cured by bad and good spirits. Medicine men were people who could work with the spirit world.

(b) Read Source B and look at Source A again. Does Source B show that beliefs about the cause and cure of illness had made progress since prehistoric times (Source A)? Use your knowledge to help you to explain your answer. (5)

> **Examiner's tip** Take note of the instruction in the question to 'use your knowledge'. Do not rely just on the information in the sources. If you do, the two sources might appear to show no progress as they both show a belief in spirits. However, you will know that the Egyptians did know more about the human body and illness. For example they did believe in some natural causes and cures, and they knew something about how the body works. Explain this in your answer.
> It is also worth mentioning that it is not possible to draw definite conclusions from these two sources as we are not certain if the figure in Source A is a medicine man and nor do we know whether or not the spell in Source B was actually used by the Egyptians. In the answer below there is good use made of knowledge of the Egyptians. The answer would receive 4 marks out of 5. The final mark would be gained by making the point that definite conclusions cannot be drawn from these two sources.

Source A shows that people in prehistoric times believed that illness was caused by spirits. They used supernatural methods to cure people. Source B does not show much progress because it shows the Egyptians also believing in spirits. But the Egyptians did know more than this. They had a natural theory about what caused illness based on blockage of the channels in the body. They also used natural cures like herbs and they took a lot of trouble to stay clean.

(c) Read Source C. What breakthrough did Hippocrates make in understanding about the cause and cure of illness? Use your knowledge as well as Sources A, B and C to help you to explain your answer. (7)

> **Examiner's tip** To score full marks for this question it is important to explain not just that Hippocrates made the move from supernatural to natural explanations of illness and treatments, but also what later developments Hippocrates' ideas led to. The answer below explains both of these areas.

Hippocrates made the important breakthrough of taking people away from the idea that illness has supernatural causes and cures. He developed the Theory of the Four Humours which said that the body is made up of four humours and that people become ill when one of the humours is out of balance with the others. This could be caused by the climate or by bad diet or not enough exercise. He told people to do things in moderation to get the humours back into balance. Hippocrates also developed the method of clinical observation which made doctors examine their patients carefully. Hippocrates' ideas led to other developments like the use of the opposites by Galen. Once people knew that illness had natural causes it meant that further progress would be made. His method of careful observation was used by many other people like Paré to make further discoveries.

Answers to Unit 1

Answer	Mark

(d) Study Source D. Had there been no progress in understanding about the cause and cure of disease between the time of Hippocrates (Source C) and the time of Charles II (Source D)? Use your knowledge as well as the sources to help you to explain your answer. (10)

Examiner's tip   At first glance Sources C and D appear to show that there was no progress, in fact things appear to have regressed because in Source D they are back to supernatural beliefs as they believe the King has special powers to cure people. But the question does instruct you to use your knowledge of the history of medicine over this period and if you do this you will realise that the sources do not tell the whole story. You could explain that in Hippocrates' time many Greeks still went to the temples of Asclepios to be cured so supernatural ideas were still accepted. Also between the times of Hippocrates and Charles II in the seventeenth century there were many ups and downs in the history of medicine and there were some periods of progress. For example Paré developed new treatments based on natural beliefs.
The answer which follows would score a high mark as knowledge of the period is used alongside the sources.

The sources show that things had gone backwards because in Source D they believe the King has supernatural powers to cure people. This is less advanced than Hippocrates who believed in natural causes and cures. But it was not really as bad as that. Even in Greek times there were many people who believed in supernatural methods. They went to Asclepeia to be healed by the god Asclepios. Later in Roman times Galen developed Hippocrates' ideas and introduced the idea of the use of opposites to keep the humours in balance. Some progress was made in the Middle Ages with the use of herbs and in the Renaissance they understood a lot more about the human body through the work of Vesalius and this made supernatural beliefs about illness less likely. So some progress was made, although not a lot.

3   There is disagreement over the importance of Fleming's role in the discovery and development of penicillin.
   (a) Briefly describe Fleming's work. (5)

Examiner's tip   Remember that there are only 5 marks for this question and that you are instructed to answer 'briefly'. It is not an invitation to write everything you know about Fleming. Nor will the Examiner be expecting you to have covered every aspect of Fleming's work. The important thing is to describe several specific aspects of his work rather than writing a general answer which could describe the work of almost anyone, e.g. 'Fleming was a very important person in the history of medicine and made many important discoveries like penicillin.' The answer which follows describes some specific aspects of his work and would receive full marks.

In the First World War Fleming had to treat wounded soldiers. He was so upset by their suffering and by the fact that antiseptics did not stop infection in many wounds that he decided to find something that would. After the war he experimented on the germs that turned wounds septic. One day he noticed that on one of his dishes the germs had stopped growing. On this dish was a mould which was producing penicillin which was killing the germs.

Answers to Unit 1

Answer	Mark

(b) Explain why penicillin was not developed before the 1940s. (7)

> **Examiner's tip** Note that this question is asking you to explain why penicillin was not developed before the 1940s. Don't fall into the trap of explaining its development or of going beyond 1940. The reasons you could explain include: Fleming's failure to turn the mould juice into pure penicillin, no money for further experiments, Fleming did no further work on penicillin. Remember to explain how these reasons contributed to penicillin not being developed. The following answer does this.

Penicillin was not developed before the 1940s because although Fleming had discovered it he was not able to produce pure penicillin which was what was needed if it was to be used as a drug. To have done this Fleming needed more money but his application for a grant was turned down. Fleming was not a chemist and did not have the skills to do the necessary work on the mould juice. Because he did not have the money he could not pay some chemists to do the work for him. Because of this failure he assumed that penicillin had no practical purpose and he lost interest in it.

(c) 'The following were all equally important reasons why penicillin was developed:
  (i) the work of Fleming;
  (ii) the work of Florey and Chain;
  (iii) chance;
  (iv) the Second World War.'

  Do you agree with this statement? Refer in your answer to (i), (ii), (iii) and (iv). (8)

> **Examiner's tip** This is where you can explain why penicillin was finally successfully developed. Remember two things: explain how the different reasons in the list contributed to its development (rather than just telling the story of penicillin), and try and show how some of them are connected, e.g. Fleming and chance, or Florey and Chain and the Second World War. The answer which follows does both these things and would score full marks.

All of the reasons in the list are important. Fleming made the important first discovery and he was clever enough to notice that the penicillin mould on his dishes was killing the germs. He realised how important this was. There was some chance involved here because he did not deliberately grow the mould. It grew on the dish because the dish had not been washed. The mould could have easily been missed when the dish was washed. But when Fleming did see the mould and the fact that there were no germs around it he realised the importance of this. Florey and Chain were very important because they started to work on penicillin again. They produced pure penicillin and tried it out on a human patient but they could not produce enough to make it any use. When the Second World War broke out and when America entered the war the American government gave Florey and some drug companies enough money to produce large quantities of penicillin. It was used on thousands of soldiers. The American government only found the money because its own soldiers were dying in the war.

Answers to Unit 2

2 DEPTH STUDY: ELIZABETHAN ENGLAND

Answer	Mark

1 (a) Study Sources A, B and C. How far do these sources fully explain why theatres were popular in the Elizabethan period? (5)

> **Examiner's tip** The important word in this question is 'fully'. You will receive reasonable marks by explaining that details in the sources such as bear-baiting and the seating arrangements (with special places for all the different classes) made the theatre popular, but the top mark will be reserved for answers which go on and explain that there were other reasons. Just one extra reason for the popularity of the theatre will do, for example the way in which playwrights made sure there was something in their plays to appeal to all classes and all levels of education. The answer given below gets no further than explaining the points in the sources and so would receive 4 marks out of 5.

Yes, these sources do explain why the theatre was popular. People enjoyed events like the bear-baiting in Source A. Source B shows that the theatres were designed so that the rich had expensive seats high up with good views but there was also a place for the poor. They stood on the ground and were called 'groundlings'. It cost just one penny to stand here. Most people could afford this.

(b) Study Source C. Did problems such as those mentioned in this source make Elizabeth close all theatres? Use your knowledge of the period to explain your answer. (7)

> **Examiner's tip** You must use your knowledge of the period to help you answer this question (note the instruction to this effect in the question). If you just base your answer on the information in Source C you will probably say that Elizabeth would close all theatres because of the noise, the vagrants and the spreading of disease. This will not be a very good answer. However, if you use your knowledge of the period you will be able to explain that Elizabeth would probably have mixed feelings about this petition. She loved the theatre and would not want to close them down, but she also had a responsibility as Queen to maintain law and order and to make sure that disease did not spread. The answer below would receive full marks.

I am not sure if Elizabeth would close down all theatres. She would not want to do this because she liked the theatre and went to performances. She also invited actors to perform at Court. But Elizabeth also had to keep law and order. Sometimes there was a lot of crime and general disorder at the theatres and this would worry her. Also the plague could be spread at theatres because large numbers of people were gathered together. When the plague was bad Elizabeth would close the theatres but she would do this reluctantly.

(c) Study Source C. 'A member of the Common Council of London and a Puritan would not have reacted to this request in the same way.' Use your knowledge of the period to explain whether or not you agree with this statement. (8)

Answers to Unit 2

Answer	Mark

> **Examiner's tip** To answer this question well you should explain why Puritans disliked the theatre so much. There are several reasons for this as you can see in the answer below. So it is likely that a Puritan would have agreed with the request to stop the theatre from being opened. The Common Council was the body which governed London. It had the responsibility for keeping law and order and for preventing disease spreading in London. So a member of the Common Council would also be worried about this new theatre but for different reasons from a Puritan. The answer below shows a good knowledge of Puritan beliefs and the responsibilities of the Common Council and would score full marks.

They might react in the same way. The Puritans were against theatres for religious and moral reasons. They thought that some of the plots in the plays were immoral and did not like men dressing up as women. They also thought that people would go to the theatre instead of going to church, and that theatres encouraged pickpockets and prostitutes. The member of the Common Council would be more worried about the fear that great crowds gathered at the theatre and this could help spread the plague. The authorities in Elizabethan times were also worried whenever large numbers of people gathered together as this could lead to a riot. So they would both agree with the request, but for different reasons.

2 (a) **Source A is only a drawing. Does this mean that it cannot be trusted as evidence about the execution of Mary, Queen of Scots? Explain your answer. (5)**

> **Examiner's tip** It is important to use your knowledge about the execution of Mary to check whether or not the drawing can be trusted. The answer given below does this. Answers which do not use knowledge in this way will get lower marks, for example 'it is not reliable because it would have been drawn from memory and some of the details would have been forgotten.'

No, this does not mean it cannot be trusted. I know that Elizabeth made sure the execution was in public so it was an example to everyone and to prove to the Catholics that Mary was really dead. This would stop them from thinking Mary was the real queen of England. The drawing shows the public watching the execution so it is reliable.

(b) **What were the disadvantages in keeping Mary, Queen of Scots a prisoner? (6)**

> **Examiner's tip** There are two possible approaches to this question and both are valid. You could explain that keeping Mary a prisoner for so long instead of having her executed meant that she could still be used by Catholics as a figurehead for a rebellion, she could still be seen as the rightful Queen of England. Or you could explain how the imprisoning of Mary annoyed Catholics in England and the Pope so much that they took action against Elizabeth. The answer which follows takes the second approach. It is a particularly good answer because it shows how some of the factors were linked, e.g. Mary's imprisonment caused the Pope to excommunicate Elizabeth, this in turn led to Catholics plotting her overthrow.

46

Answers to Unit 2

Answer	Mark

The main disadvantage was that it made the Pope excommunicate Elizabeth in 1570 and announce that Catholics should no longer recognise Elizabeth as the rightful Queen. This meant that Catholics were able to go ahead and plot against Elizabeth and a year later there was the Ridolfi Plot. The Pope's action also encouraged Philip of Spain to plan to invade England because he thought he was doing it for his religion.

(c) Were the English Catholics a serious threat to Elizabeth? Support your answer with reasons and examples. (9)

> **Examiner's tip** Here you are being asked to reach a judgement about whether or not the English Catholics were really a serious threat to Elizabeth. Make sure you do not give a general answer. The question does instruct you to support your answer with reasons and examples and you must do this. The answer which follows is a good one because it gives reasons, supported with specific examples, why the Catholics can be seen both as a serious threat and as not much of a threat. The answer ends with an overall conclusion about how serious the threat really was. Make sure you do not write about the Pope or Philip of Spain. This question is just about English Catholics (this does include the Jesuits who came to England – they were English).

In some ways the English Catholics were not much of a threat. Most Catholics in England were happy to recognise Elizabeth as the rightful Queen and they supported her. Most did not take part in any plots against her. They just quietly worshipped as Catholics and did not cause any trouble. But some were more of a threat. The Jesuits like Campion who secretly travelled around the country were a danger because they won people back to the Catholic Church and kept their spirits up. Also there were some attempted rebellions like the Northern Rebellion which was supported by powerful nobles in the north. But the rebellions and plots were dealt with quite easily. Overall, the Catholics were not much of a threat because most of them stayed loyal to Elizabeth.

(d) How important were Mary, Queen of Scots' own actions in bringing about her execution? Support your answer with reasons and examples. (10)

> **Examiner's tip** This question is asking you to compare the importance of Mary's actions with other factors in bringing about her execution. This means that you must explain both Mary's own actions, then other factors, and then reach a conclusion about which were the more important. The answer which follows does all of this.

Mary's situation was made much worse by other people. The Pope by excommunicating Elizabeth encouraged Catholics to rebel against her. This made Mary much more of a danger and made her execution more likely. Philip of Spain also claimed that Mary was the rightful Queen instead of Elizabeth. Mary was not involved in the Northern Rebellion at all. In fact she was against it. So none of these things were Mary's fault, and they all made her execution more likely. But she did make things worse for herself. She was involved in the Ridolfi Plot and she was trapped into agreeing to Babington's plot to assassinate Elizabeth. I think that the actions of other people were more important than Mary's own actions but she did help to make her situation worse.

Answers to Unit 2

Answer	Mark

3 (a) Briefly describe the life led by vagrants in Elizabethan England. (5)

> **Examiner's tip** Do not spend too long on this question. It is only worth 5 marks and is not asking you to write everything you know about vagrants. The question does ask for a brief answer, and a few specific points about the way of life of vagrants will do. Make sure your answer relates to vagrants in Elizabethan times and does not give a general account which could be about vagrants at any time in the past. The answer given below is a very good one and would receive full marks.

Vagrants wandered from place to place sometimes in large groups. These large groups could terrorise a village but more often they just begged and stole things as they moved about the countryside. Some of these people were genuinely incapable of work such as the disabled but some deliberately avoided doing any kind of work. If they were caught they could be whipped or branded and they would be sent back to the parish where they were born.

(b) In what ways were attitudes of the councils in towns such as Ipswich and Norwich towards the poor both different from and similar to the attitudes of the Elizabethan government? (7)

> **Examiner's tip** The important point to explain is that in the early part of the reign the towns had a very different approach towards the poor from that of the government. Later in the reign, however, the government started to pass laws which were based on what some of the towns had been doing for some time. The basic difference between the two at the beginning of the reign was that the government treated all the poor as the same, whereas some of the town councils tried to distinguish between the deserving poor – who they tried to help, and those who were just idle – who they punished. The answer which follows covers all of these points.

Towns like Ipswich and Norwich punished anyone who was deliberately avoiding work, but they realised that some people who were poor and unemployed could not help it. Genuine beggars were given licences allowing them to beg. Bridewells were set up where people were given work to do. Orphaned children and children from poor homes were given an education and trained in a trade. But the idle poor were arrested and punished. All of this was paid for by raising local rates. At first the national government just passed harsher and harsher punishments for vagabonds. They thought that all poor people were the same. They thought that it was wicked to be poor. But eventually they realised that the poor had to be put into different groups and some should be helped. At the end of the reign the Elizabethan Poor Law was passed. This applied to every parish. Everyone had to pay rates and the money was used to help the deserving poor.

(c) 'The following were all equally important reasons for the large numbers of poor and unemployed in Elizabethan England:
  (i) agricultural enclosures;
  (ii) the rising population;

Answers to Unit 3

Answer	Mark

(iii) rising prices;
(iv) idleness.'
Do you agree with this statement? Refer in your answer to (i), (ii), (iii) and (iv). (8)

Examiner's tip You are not simply being asked to write about each of these reasons. You have to explain whether or not they were equally important in causing poverty. There are two ways of doing this. You can either explain how one was more important than the others (make sure you compare them all; do not just write about the one you think is most important) or you can explain how it is difficult to say that one is more important because they are all linked to each other (make sure you explain how they are linked). Remember, there is not one correct answer to this question. You are being asked for your opinion. But you must be able to support it with evidence from the period. See if you can tell which approach the answer which follows has adopted.

It is difficult to say which of these was the most important reason because they are all connected to each other. One could not have happened without the other. For example, prices did go up very fast and to make matters worse the basic food that people had to buy to stay alive went up the fastest. This made life very hard for many people. One of the reasons why food prices were going up was the large rise in population at this time. So these two factors are connected and you cannot really say that one is more important than the other. The rise in population also meant that there were more people after jobs, so the number of unemployed went up. Enclosures did not help. This was when farmers converted land from arable to pasture. So instead of growing crops they kept animals. This meant that people who had rented land were thrown off the land and replaced by sheep. This made the situation even worse with even more people poor. I don't think idleness was an important cause. There were some people who were lazy but most people wanted a job but could not get one because of the rise in population and because of enclosures.

3 DEPTH STUDY: BRITAIN, 1815–51

Answer	Mark

1 (a) **Study Sources A and B. How do Sources A and B help us to understand the problems of poverty in British towns in the middle of the 19th century?** (5)

Examiner's tip It is important to do two things in your answer. First you must use the sources to find examples of the poverty people suffered at this time. This is fairly straightforward and there are many examples you could use. Two or three will be sufficient. Secondly, you should add that these two sources do not help us to understand everything about poverty at that time. For example, the sources do not tell us anything about the causes of poverty. Nor do they tell us how widespread it was, they just give us two examples. The answer given below would receive full marks.

Answers to Unit 3

Answer	Mark

Source A shows the terrible housing conditions of the poor. The housing shown is overcrowded and dark. There is little fresh air and rubbish would collect in the drains. Source B tells us that they had little money to buy food and so had a poor, unhealthy diet and little to eat. They would also find it difficult to keep warm in the winter. Towards the end of the week they ran out of money and could not buy anything. The sources do not tell us how many people in the country suffered like this. These two sources might not be typical of most people.

(b) Read Source C and study Source D. What are the main differences between the ways of life of the well-off families in Sources C and D, and the poor people in Sources A and B? (6)

> **Examiner's tip** Do not try to describe every difference of detail. This would take you far too long and there are only six marks for this question. Instead, try and say something about different aspects of life. For example you could give examples of differences in some of the following areas: quality of diet, leisure and lifestyle, clothes, material possessions.

There are lots of differences. The rich family has a varied diet with lots of different foods like meat, fish, butter, vegetables, eggs and fruit. This is a healthy diet. The poor family eat almost the same thing every day – potatoes, and have no meat. They have no fruit. The rich family also have a lot more food.

The mother in the poor family has to work as hard as she can at cleaning and brushmaking to keep her family fed while the rich family have servants to do all their work for them. This gives them more leisure time. They spend £65 a year on their horses while the poor family has a yearly income of £8 a year. The rich family are well dressed and can obviously afford good clothes. The poor families are dressed in rags.

(c) Which TWO of Sources A, B, C, and D would you choose as the most reliable to show the differences between the lives of rich and poor in Britain in the first half of the 19th century? Use your knowledge of the period to help you to explain why you have chosen these sources. (8)

> **Examiner's tip** There is no one right answer to this question. It does not matter which two sources you choose. What does matter are the reasons you give for your choice. Your reasons should refer to how complete a picture of the differences between rich and poor the sources give us. You should use your knowledge of the period when you are making judgements about the sources. The answer below judges the completeness of the sources and uses knowledge of the period.

Source A is a photograph of just one street at one point in time and Source B is just about one family. Source B is very reliable about this one family but we do not know how typical this family was. Sources C and D are probably more reliable. Source C appears to be a picture of a typical wealthy family at this time and would contain evidence taken from a number of households. It is not about a real family but is made up to show what a typical rich family was like. Source D is probably similar. The artist has gathered together information about well-off families and has then drawn this picture giving an overall view of rich families. These two sources would therefore be reliable about the differences between rich and poor. Many of the families who moved

Answers to Unit 3

Answer	Mark

into towns at this time lived in dreadful conditions. The houses were overcrowded and damp and there was no clean water or proper sewers. A widow like the one in Source B would struggle. She had no regular job and there would be no poor relief for her unless she went into a workhouse. Even families with both parents out working often struggled to keep going. So Source B is not completely typical but does give a fairly reliable view of the living standards of poor people at this time.

(d) Read Source E. Does Source E give enough evidence to explain why there was such a gap between the lives of the rich and the poor? Use Sources A, B, C, D and E and your knowledge of the period to help you to explain your answer. (9)

> **Examiner's tip** Source E does provide some reasons why there was such a gap between rich and poor and you should explain these. However, there are some things that are not explained by Source E, for example the growing gap between agricultural workers and land-owners. You need to use your own knowledge to explain that this is something that is missing from Source E. The answer which follows would score full marks. It begins by explaining what Source E does tell us and then it moves on to explain some of the things Source E does not tell us.

Source E does give some evidence why there was a large gap between rich and poor. It explains that some working people were put out of work by the new machines. Those that did work in the factories often lived in terrible housing conditions where there was overcrowding and dirt and damp which spread diseases like cholera. The middle classes who owned the factories, however, made fortunes out of this industrialisation. The source only explains about the situation in the towns. It does not explain about the countryside where the labourers were very badly off. They lost the outdoor poor relief which they had got under the Old Poor Law. The price of food was going up very quickly and the new threshing machines put a lot of people out of work. The landowners did very well by keeping the price of their corn high.

(e) Read Source F and read Source E again. Why do you think that Sources E and F give different interpretations of the effects of the changes in Britain during the first half of the 19th century? Use your knowledge of the period to help you to explain your answer. (10)

> **Examiner's tip** These two sources do give different impressions of the effects of the changes in Britain in the first half of the nineteenth century. Source E concentrates on the poor and the largely negative effects of the changes while Source F is more hopeful and suggests that even for those who have not done well there are the colonies where they can go and make a fresh start. The question is asking you to suggest possible reasons why they give these different impressions. Do not give general answers such as, 'they used different sources'. It is important to look at when the sources were written. Source E was written recently and because of our attitudes today is more likely to condemn the plight of the poor than someone at the time. Source F was written by a Victorian who will be less interested in the poor and more likely to praise his own society. The answer below makes these points well.

The author of Source E is writing in the 1980s. Today we are more interested in the poor and we would be horrified by the dreadful conditions many people had to suffer in

51

Answers to Unit 3

Answer	Mark

the nineteenth century. This is why the author concentrates on the overcrowding, the dirt, the unemployed and the disease. The author of Source F was writing at the time and will be proud of Victorian Britain and will concentrate on the good things. He also has a good opinion of the colonies which is typical of the time when they regarded the Empire as a great achievement. Today we are more critical of the effects of the Empire.

(f) Read Sources E and F again. Sources E and F mention two ways in which the problems of poverty were dealt with at the time. How useful do you find these sources to explain why people went to workhouses or emigrated? Use your knowledge of the period to help you to explain your answer. (10)

> **Examiner's tip** In answering this question you should try and do two things. First, test the sources for accuracy – use what you know about the period to test whether or not what they say about why people went into workhouses or emigrated is right. Second, use your knowledge of the period to decide whether or not there are other reasons why people went into workhouses or emigrated which are not mentioned in these two sources. The answer below would receive full marks as it adopts both of these approaches.

These sources are quite useful. What Source E says about why people went into workhouses is quite right. Since the introduction of the New Poor Law in 1834 anyone who could not support themselves had to go into the workhouse as outdoor relief was no longer allowed. Some of those were skilled workers who were put out of work by the new machines. However Source E does not mention other reasons why people went into workhouses. For example in the north of England people were put out of work for short periods by a slump in trade. Source F is useful because it is right when it tells us that younger sons of landed families often emigrated to make their fortune overseas. But it doesn't mention that most people who emigrated were poor and desperate like the people in Ireland after the Irish Potato Famine in the 1840s or the people in Scotland after the Highland Clearances when they were turned off the land.

(g) Study Source G and read Source F again. Sources F and G suggest that emigration was more successful than the workhouses in dealing with the problems of poverty in Britain. Do you agree? Use your knowledge of the period to help you to explain your answer. (12)

> **Examiner's tip** As with the last question there should be two parts to your answer. First you should evaluate the two sources for reliability. Then you should use your knowledge of the workhouses and emigration to discuss whether you think that emigration was more successful than the workhouses in dealing with the problem of poverty. Remember that both emigration and workhouses had advantages and disadvantages and you should try and write a balanced answer pointing these out. Do not be too one-sided, although at the end of your answer you can finally come down on one side or the other. The answer which follows would score full marks.

Source F certainly suggests that emigration was very successful. But it was written in the nineteenth century and the author really has not had the time to see whether

Answers to Unit 3

Answer	Mark

or not most people who emigrated were successful. Also the author is biased, he obviously thinks the Empire and emigration are good. What he does not mention are the many people who emigrated and failed. Generally people who went in organised parties like those from the Petworth estate did well. But those who went out by themselves without making many arrangements did find life very hard. They could not find jobs and ended up in poverty. Some of those from the Highland Clearances in Scotland who went to Canada ended up like this. Of course, many of the poor did not emigrate at all and so emigration did not deal with the majority of the poor. The workhouses were opposed at first as Source G shows. This opposition was strongest in the north where unemployment was usually temporary and it was silly to send people to a workhouse for a few months every year. Many refused to go. So it could be said that the workhouses did not help the problem of poverty. But many people argued that under the old system many people deliberately avoided work because they knew they could get out-door relief. The workhouses were so dreadful that people often did find work to avoid going into them and the poor rates went down suggesting they were successful. But the system was still based on the idea that it was a person's own fault that they were poor when many people could not help it. Both emigration and the workhouses helped a bit but neither solved the problem. There was still a big problem of poverty.

2 (a) **Briefly describe the main criticisms of the electoral system before 1832.** (5)

> **Examiner's tip** Remember that you are not being asked to write everything you know about the electoral system. The question does say 'briefly describe' and all you are expected to do for full marks is to describe three or four main criticisms. Make them specific, as the answer below does, and avoid general answers, e.g. 'it was unfair and a lot of people thought it should be changed.'

The main criticisms were that only a few people were allowed to vote and who was allowed to vote changed from one constituency to another. In some 'pocket boroughs' there were only a handful of voters and they were controlled by the landowner. There was a lot of bribery with people selling their votes. There were too many constituencies in the south leaving all the new industrial towns in the north under-represented. The main complaint was that the middle classes who produced Britain's wealth often did not have the vote and there were few of them in Parliament.

(b) **How far was the electoral system improved by the 1832 Reform Act? Explain your answer.** (7)

> **Examiner's tip** In answering this question you need to explain some of the ways in which the electoral system was improved and some of the ways in which it was not improved. Then you need to reach an overall judgement about 'how far' it was improved. Do not claim that every wrong with the old system was put right in 1832 because it was not. And do not claim that a secret ballot was introduced (this was not introduced until 1872). The answer below would receive full marks as it covers improvements, areas not improved, and reaches an overall conclusion.

Answers to Unit 3

Answer | Mark

The system was improved by giving more people the vote. The middle classes were given the vote and now about 1 in 5 people could vote instead of 1 in 10. In boroughs standard rules about who could vote were introduced. The north of England was given more seats and lots of rotten boroughs in the south and west of the country were abolished. Towns like Leeds and Manchester had their own M.P. for the first time. But there were some things that were not improved. People still had to vote in public so they could be threatened and bribed about who they voted for. There were still a lot of pocket boroughs in the control of a landowner left and the large towns in the north still did not have enough M.P.s. M.P.s were still not paid and so it was difficult for working-class people to become M.P.s. Overall the system was changed to let the middle classes in, but most of the people, the working classes, were kept out.

(c) 'The following were all equally important reasons why the Reform Act was passed in 1832:
   (i) support for reform from the middle classes;
   (ii) working-class riots, 1830–1832;
   (iii) fear of revolution;
   (iv) the activities of radicals such as Francis Place.'
   Do you agree with this statement? Refer in your answer to (i), (ii), (iii) and (iv). (8)

Examiner's tip It is important that you write about at least three of the reasons in the list. Do not just write about the one you think is the most important. You can argue either that they were equally important or that one was more important or less important than the others. What matters are the reasons you give. If you are arguing they were all equally important try and explain the connections between them, e.g. the riots led to fears of revolution. If you are trying to argue that one was more or less important than the others you must compare the different reasons and show how they varied in importance. The answer which follows explains the connections between the different reasons and argues that one was not more important than the others because they all depended on each other.

All of these reasons were important because they were all connected. The support of the middle classes was very important because they were respectable and the ruling class did not fear them. They were rich factory owners and very wealthy. They were responsible for the wealth of the country and they had a very strong case for being given the vote. The middle classes thought reform was needed because if there was no reform there might be a revolution like in France. This fear was increased by the working-class riots. These riots like the one in Bristol showed everyone that something had to be done. But they had no intention of giving the working classes the vote as they might take over. The Whigs believed the best thing to do was pass a small reform which would let the middle classes in. The system would still be in the hands of wealthy people not the rabble. So all of these reasons made them pass small reforms to stop something worse happening.

Answers to Unit 4

4 DEPTH STUDY: THE AMERICAN WEST, 1840–95

Answer   **Mark**

1 (a) **What were the dangers and difficulties of trail life?** (6)

> **Examiner's tip** Some dangers and difficulties can be seen in the sources – for example, Indians and mountains – and you can use these in your answer. However, if you are to earn full marks, your answer must also include other factors not covered by the sources – remember that the question has instructed you to use the sources and your own knowledge in your answer. The following answer would have scored full marks.

Source A shows some of the problems of trail life. The emigrants were in danger of being attacked by Indians. The ground they were crossing was often very rough, and the oxen pulling the wagons had to be forced to pull the wagons up steep slopes. Source B shows that the trails were very long and they had to go through the Rocky Mountains, which were difficult to cross, and where the weather might be very bad. There were other problems too, like getting food and water both for themselves and for the animals. Sometimes the wagons might break down, and then they would have to mend them with whatever tools and materials they had available. If anyone fell ill, there would be no doctor to look after them.

(b) **Why were settlers willing to make such a hard and long journey?** (7)

> **Examiner's tip** There were lots of reasons why people moved west, but they were of two types – dissatisfaction with the life they had (push factors) and reasons for believing that life in the west would be better (pull factors). A good answer, like the one below, will deal with both types, and quote several specific reasons.

Settlers would not have gone west if they did not expect life to be better once they got there. Good land was becoming scarcer in the east as more and more immigrants arrived from Europe. Many of the immigrants had been farmers back home, and they could not settle in the cities of the east. Some groups like the Mormons were persecuted for their religion so moved to find somewhere they could practise their religion as they wished. Reports of good land to be had in the west, particularly in Oregon, encouraged people to move. This became a flood of people during the California gold rush as people heard stories of fortunes to be made. The people who had gone west would then write to their families and encourage them to move too.

Answers to Unit 4

Answer	Mark

(c) **Why was the far west settled before the Great Plains?** (7)

> **Examiner's tip** Again, there are many reasons why the far west was settled before the Great Plains, but a good answer must not just deal with why settlers were attracted to the far west first, it must also explain why the Great Plains were less attractive. In other words, your answer must compare the advantages and disadvantages of the two areas, as in the following example.

The Great Plains were known as 'the Great American Desert'. Farming there was not easy. The climate was harsh, with hot summers and cold winters, there was not much water, and there was little wood for fuel and fencing. The land was inhabited by Indians who were prepared to resist settlers. In other words you would have to be desperate for land to want to settle there. The far west was different. Much of the land there was fertile, there was plenty of water in most areas, and it could be reached by sea, which made it easier to get hold of supplies. The gold rush also gave people a reason for going to California. It was only later, when pressure for land increased and new crops and inventions made farming on the Plains more possible, that large numbers of settlers went there.

2 (a) **Study Source A. What attitude do you think the person who drew Source A had to the role of women homesteaders on the Great Plains?** (4)

> **Examiner's tip** The difficulty here is to focus your answer on the artist's attitude, rather than on what he shows as the women's role, which is to cook and look after the children. Because he does not indicate any criticism of what is going on, we can infer that he does not disapprove of the roles of the men and women. But the scene is idealised; that is, it is not realistic and paints a rosy picture of life on the Plains. For a start, usually there was not enough wood to build a log cabin, and they had to build sod houses. So whatever his attitude was, it was not based on any understanding of what life was really like for the homesteaders. Any answer making these points would gain full marks, as in the example below.

The attitude of the artist towards the women's role is not really clear. He seems to approve of the fact that the women are doing the cooking while the men build the cabin. Probably, like most people at the time, he thought that each sex had its own work to do. But we cannot be sure this is really his attitude towards women homesteaders because the picture is so unrealistic. Everyone looks happy, well dressed and well fed. Life on the Plains was much tougher than this.

(b) **Read Sources B and C. Explain the different attitudes towards women on the Great Plains shown in Sources B and C.** (6)

Answers to Unit 4

Answer	Mark

> **Examiner's tip** First, you must identify the attitudes towards women shown in each source, and then you must explain why people had these attitudes. The following answer deals well with both sources.

The two sources show different attitudes. Source B shows respect for women and Source C shows lack of respect. The writer of Source B is obviously shocked by the behaviour of women in Wichita, which was a cow town in the 1860s, so many of the women he is writing about were probably bar-girls and prostitutes, which explains their behaviour. In Source C the woman is more civilized than the men who are interviewing her. They are used to the rough life of the Plains, including going to the toilet behind the nearest tree. They think someone who wants a proper toilet is just causing trouble, which shows their lack of respect for better standards of behaviour.

(c) **Would women have welcomed their new lives on the Great Plains? Use your own knowledge and Sources A, B and C to help you explain your answer.** (10)

> **Examiner's tip** This is an empathy question. It is asking you about the attitudes of women on the Great Plains as a group, and a good answer will first look for ways of identifying and explaining different attitudes within the group. It is a mistake to imagine that everyone within a group has the same feelings, beliefs or motives. But the best answers will go beyond this; they will show an awareness that individuals sometimes have mixed feelings, perhaps they aren't sure what they feel, or perhaps their feelings change with time. These answers show that people's feelings are complex and cannot always be explained in straightforward terms. Lastly, the question tells you to use the sources and your own knowledge. To gain full marks you need to do both, as in the answer below.

For many homesteaders life on the Plains was very hard. Women probably hoped for a new and better life when they moved to the Plains – some found a better life and some did not. Those that got a homestead with reasonable land, where they could make a proper farm, probably did welcome their new lives. Those that worked hard for years only to be driven off their farms by drought or locusts probably felt bitter about it all. Homesteaders weren't the only women on the Plains, though. The sources show that the opening up of the Plains gave employment to women. The schoolteacher in Source C might have been a bit shocked by the conditions, but she was probably glad of the job. For almost all women, things got easier as time went by. Towns were built, it got easier to buy supplies, people weren't so isolated once railways were built. Plenty of women probably thought the Plains were horrible when they first went, but if they stayed long enough, they saw civilization arrive.

Answers to Unit 4

Answer	Mark

3 (a) **Briefly explain what the US government and white Americans meant when they talked about the 'Indian problem' in the West.** (5)

> **Examiner's tip** Take note of the word 'briefly'. You could write a great deal about the 'Indian problem', but with only five marks at stake you should limit your answer to a couple of paragraphs at most. Another important word in the question is 'explain'. This means that not only will you have to state what the 'Indian problem' was, but also you will have explain *why* it was a problem. Saying that the problem was that the Indians lived on the Plains and the whites wanted the land is enough to identify the problem, but pointing out that the whites wanted the land for farming, for ranching or for mining, and that this caused disputes between the whites and the Indians, is also providing some explanation. There are other ways of explaining the problem. For example, you could mention that Indians had been promised certain parts of the Plains, or that the Indians were good fighters and would resist attempts to take away their land. Any answer like the example below, which *identifies* what the 'Indian problem' was, and *explains* why it was a problem, giving a couple of reasons, would certainly receive full marks.

The 'Indian problem' was that the Indians had something which the whites wanted – the land of the Great Plains. Once all the good farming land in the East was used up, settlers started moving on to the Plains, and this brought them into contact with the Plains Indians. The situation got worse when gold was discovered in the Black Hills which was a sacred area to the Sioux. The government had promised they could keep this area for ever, and now miners wanted to go there. This was a problem because the Indians would fight to protect their land, and the government would have to decide what to do about it. Some people and politicians wanted to put the Indians on reservations, others simply wanted to wipe all the Indians out.

(b) **Explain why many Plains Indians found it difficult to live on the reservations.** (7)

> **Examiner's tip** This question requires you to use your understanding of the way of life and attitudes of the Plains Indians to explain why they objected to living on reservations. In questions which ask 'Why?', never give just one reason. Try to think of several. Then you must explain why each of these reasons was significant – why it mattered to those involved. Given that the question carries seven marks, it would be reasonable to assume that if you could explain three reasons why the Indians hated the reservations, you would be bound to score a high mark.

The Indians found it difficult to live on reservations because it was impossible to carry on their traditional way of life. For example they could not go hunting. Before they were forced onto reservations, the Indians had been nomadic, roaming over the Plains and

Answers to Unit 4

Answer | Mark

following the herds of buffalo which they hunted. Now they had to stay in the small area of the reservation. In any case, most of the buffalo were killed by white hunters (**first reason explained**). So to get food, the whites tried to encourage them to farm, but most tribes had no idea how to grow crops, and anyway the reservations usually had all the worst land, so many tribes had to depend on handouts of food (**second reason explained**). Many whites hoped that life on the reservation would 'civilise' the Indians – they set up schools and churches, and tried to break down the tribal way of life with respect for the chiefs – but the Indians realised that they were being forced to lose their own culture and beliefs (**third reason explained**).

(c) **Was the moving of the Plains Indians onto reservations the only reason why the white Americans were able to destroy the Indian way of life? Explain your answer.** (8)

> **Examiner's tip** Don't fall into the trap of agreeing with the idea that reservations were the only reason. Events in history always have many causes, so here you must deny that reservations were the only reason, and explain what the other reasons were. This does not mean that you can ignore the impact of the reservations – this must be analysed as part of your answer. The best approach, however, is to construct an explanation which shows how the different reasons contributed *together* to destroying the Indians' way of life. In other words, you should show how the reasons were *linked*. Finally, as mentioned in the first two parts of this question, don't be satisfied just with giving a reason; always *explain* that reason too. For example, one student might write, 'No, it wasn't reservations, it was that the whites had killed all the buffalo.' This is true, but it is not an explanation because it does not tell us *why* and *how* killing the buffalo led to the destruction of the Indians' way of life.

It is true that Indians living on reservations could not lead their traditional way of life. The whites wanted to keep them under control. They did not want them wandering around the Plains causing trouble with white settlers. So they tried to turn the Indians into white people by making them live a settled life. They wanted the Indians to be farmers, not hunters and warriors.

However, it was not reservations which destroyed the Indians' way of life. They would not have agreed to go onto reservations in the first place if they thought they had any chance of keeping their old way of life. Most tribes understood they had little choice, so in deciding why the whites could destroy the Indians' way of life, you have really got to explain what it was that made the Indians agree to go on to reservations. (**This paragraph analyses the role of the reservations.**)

The basic reason was that the Indians were defeated. Although they had the odd success like the Little Bighorn, the Indians did not have any chance of finally defeating the whites. They were outnumbered, and the whites had modern technology on their

Answers to Unit 4

Answer — Mark

side. If they did not agree to go onto reservations, they would die. The most important factor in defeating the Indians was the destruction of the buffalo herds. The white hunters deliberately slaughtered the buffalo. This robbed the Indians of most of what they needed to exist. The way of life of the Plains Indians was totally dependent on the buffalo; without it, they had no way to survive except by going onto reservations. There are other reasons too. The construction of the railways opened up the Plains. Large numbers of white people – miners, farmers, hunters, cattlemen – could now settle and work in an area which previously no whites had wanted. The railways made the Plains accessible, and this made it inevitable that the whites would have to deal with the 'Indian problem'. The railways brought the hunters who shot the buffalo in such huge numbers. They brought the settlers who took over the land. They made cattle ranching profitable, as now the cattle could be shipped back East. (**This paragraph considers other reasons.**)

All these reasons played a part in destroying the Indians' way of life. If the railways had not existed, the whites would not have wanted the land of the Plains. If they hadn't wanted the Plains, the buffalo would not have been shot. If the buffalo had not been shot, the Indians could have carried on with their way of life. The reservations carried on the process of destroying the Indians' way of life, but they were not the main reason for it. (**This paragraph shows how the reasons were linked.**)

5 DEPTH STUDY: GERMANY, 1919–45

Answer — Mark

1 (a) Briefly describe Hitler's main political ideas. (5)

> **Examiner's tip** Take note of the word 'briefly'. The problem here is selecting what to write about, and judging how much to write. Given that only five marks are available, you should think of writing no more than a paragraph. Hitler had many different political ideas, such as hatred of the Jews (anti-semitism), wanting to reject the Treaty of Versailles, wanting to unite all Germans in one country, planning to destroy German democracy, and so on. You are not expected to write in detail about all of them. The examiners decided that anyone who could identify and describe three ideas would be given full marks. The following answer describes more than three ideas, but does it quite briefly in a single paragraph. It would certainly score full marks.

Hitler had many ideas, most of them based on hating someone or something. He hated the Jews, and blamed them for making Germany weak and for Germany's defeat in the First World War. He believed that the pure Germans (the Aryans) were a kind of master-race who would rule the world, so naturally he believed all other races were inferior. He wanted to keep the German race pure, which in the end led him to try and wipe out other races like the Jews. He also wanted to make Germany great again. When he came to power he simply ignored the Treaty of Versailles, and built up Germany's armed forces again. He thought Germany should expand into other countries to gain living space (lebensraum) for the true Germans, and to conquer all

Answers to Unit 5

Answer	Mark

those areas of Europe where Germans lived. Finally he believed that he should be the supreme ruler, which meant he would tolerate no opposition. He hated democracy, and when he came to power he arrested or murdered all his opponents.

(b) In what ways were the aims of the Weimar governments, 1919–33, both different from and similar to those of Hitler's government? (7)

> **Examiner's tip** You may again face problems of selecting your material in this question. There were many similarities and differences between the aims of the Weimar and the Hitler governments. You cannot expect to cover them all in an answer of a couple of paragraphs. If you can think of three similarities and three differences this would almost certainly give you ample material. The really important point, though, is that your answer must deal both with similarity and difference, as the question instructs. Good answers will do more than simply identify similarities and differences; they will also explain them. So simply stating, say, that the Weimar government wanted to establish democracy, and Hitler did not, would get you some credit for identifying a difference. But explaining that Weimar governments were based on democratic principles, were freely elected and tried to create freedom and justice for German people, whilst Hitler was a cruel dictator who tried to force the German people to accept his will, would rightly be regarded as a much better approach, and would gain more marks. Certainly, if you could treat three similarities and three differences in this way you would be sure to obtain full marks. The following example does this.

Most people would say that the Weimar governments were very different from Hitler, but this is not completely true. The Weimar Republic was forced to sign the Treaty of Versailles, but they never really accepted it, and did all they could to undermine it. Hitler was more open in his opposition to the Treaty, introducing rearmament for instance, but all Germans wanted to overthrow it if they could. Even in the Locarno Pacts the Weimar government refused to guarantee Germany's eastern frontiers; this is not so different from Hitler wanting lebensraum in the East. In domestic policy there were similarities too. Both Weimar and Hitler had to cope with serious economic problems, unemployment being the most important, though the Weimar Republic faced inflation too. So they both aimed for economic recovery, and after 1923 the Weimar Republic achieved this, and after 1933 Hitler achieved it.

But there were also very great differences between them. Hitler was a cruel dictator. He crushed all opposition. He did not believe in freedom, and used terror and concentration camps against his enemies. He aimed to dominate Germany. The Weimar Republic was a democracy. It stood for decency and freedom. People could vote for their rulers. However much the Republic opposed the Treaty of Versailles, it did not suggest going to war to put things right. It believed in getting on with other nations, and negotiating to get its way. Hitler wanted to treat international opponents the same way he treated opposition at home – by using violence, which led eventually to the war. Lastly, Hitler had crazy racial theories, and his aim was to create a German super-race. Other races, such as the Jews, were persecuted and despised. The Weimar Republic had no such ideas, and gave equality to all regardless of religion, race or sex.

(c) 'The following were all equally important reasons for Hitler's powerful position by the end of 1933:
  (i) the Treaty of Versailles;

Answers to Unit 5

Answer	Mark

    (ii) the economic crisis of 1929–33;
    (iii) the personal qualities of Hitler;
    (iv) the Enabling Act of 1933.'
Do you agree with this statement? Refer in your answer to (i), (ii), (iii) and (iv).   (8)

> **Examiner's tip**   As with other questions in this book which have given several factors for you to consider, the task is to compare these factors, and to reach a judgement about their relative importance. Many students will go through each of the given factors and explain why it was important in helping Hitler achieve power by 1933. If done thoroughly this would earn a high mark, but to get full marks you need to do a little more. The question asks whether the factors were equally important. It is inviting you to make a judgement. You might decide:
> 1. that one cause was more important than the others. If so, you will not just have to explain why your chosen cause was important, but also why the other causes were less important.
> 2. that they were all equally important. If so, you will need to explain that they were all essential, and that Hitler would not have come to power if one of these factors had been absent.
> 3. that the factors were interlinked, and so cannot be separated. If so, you will need to explain how the factors together led Hitler to power in 1933. This argument could be similar or the same as saying that they were all equally important.
>
> Any of these arguments, fully explained, could earn the full eight marks. The following example uses the third approach.

All of the causes were important in helping Hitler achieve almost total power in Germany by 1933. All Germans hated the Treaty of Versailles and wanted it overthrown. Hitler promised to do this, so the Treaty gave him useful propaganda which he could use to gain support. The unemployment caused by the Great Crash brought about a crisis for the Weimar Republic, which seemed powerless to solve mass unemployment. Hitler promised to make jobs, and many people believed him. This won him support. Hitler's personality was also vital. He was a powerful speaker and a master of propaganda. He believed in his destiny. He was determined to succeed. He was prepared to force people to obey him. He was a determined and effective leader of his Party. Obviously this helped him become a leader with a national reputation, whom people were prepared to listen to. Lastly, the Enabling Act was what gave him the legal power to do what he wanted, and rule without being restricted by the Reichstag. It made him the dictator of Germany.

What is impossible is to say that one of these causes was more important than the others. They all contributed to Hitler's rise to power, but in different ways. The Treaty of Versailles and the economic crisis gave Hitler opportunities to exploit, but without his personality he would have been just another German moaning about unemployment. On the other hand, even with his personality, if there had not been grievances for him to exploit then the Germans would never have turned to him for leadership. Finally, the Enabling Act did make him a dictator; without it he would still have been controlled by the President and the Reichstag. But it would never have been passed if Germany had not been in such a mess because of the economic and political crisis of 1929-33. So all the factors are linked together in explaining why Hitler achieved total power in Germany.

Answers to Unit 5

Answer	Mark

2 (a) Study Source A. What do you think the person who drew Source A felt about the SA? (4)

> **Examiner's tip** Your task is to interpret the cartoon, using your knowledge of the period. The best answers to the question will go beyond what the cartoon shows about the SA – that they were violent, threatening, made people fear them – and will recognize that the cartoonist is making the point that people's support for the Nazis is dependent on the fear that the SA produces. The following answer is brief, but would score full marks.

I don't think the cartoonist supported the SA. He shows them as brutal and violent. But he thinks they are important because if they weren't around threatening people, then maybe support for the Nazis would not be so strong.

(b) Read Sources B and C. Sources B and C show different attitudes towards the activities of the SA. Why do you think this is so? (6)

> **Examiner's tip** Here you must use your knowledge of the topic to explain why the author of Source B holds one view of the SA in 1926, and the author of Source C holds another view of the SA in 1933, and why their attitudes are different. It is not enough, for example, to say that the authors of the two sources are simply talking about different things – dealing with Communists in Source B, and not being policemen in Source C. You need to identify and explain the change in attitude towards the SA that has occurred between the writing of the two sources. The answer below does this well.

In 1926 Hitler was not in power. He was still struggling to make the Nazis into an important national party. He needed the SA as a private army. He knew that he would have to use violence, particularly against the Communists, and the SA would do his dirty work for him. This explains why he supports the SA in Source B. By the time Source C was written things had changed. Hitler had come to power. The SA was now an embarrassment. They wanted jobs. They thought they could behave as they wished. Most alarmingly, they wanted to be merged with the army. Hitler could not afford to lose the support of the army. Frick is trying to bring the SA under control. The SA are now a problem for the Nazis. This explains why the two sources show different attitudes towards the SA.

(c) Germans at this time had different views about the SA. Why was this so? Use your own knowledge and Sources A, B and C to help you to explain your answer. (8)

63

Answers to Unit 5

Answer — Mark

> **Examiner's tip** Note that the question tells you to use the sources and your own knowledge. This is a clear signal that using material from the sources alone will not gain full marks. This question is designed to test your ability to show empathetic understanding of people in Nazi Germany. When you are asked about the views held by groups of people the first point to bear in mind is that there will be a variety of views – not everybody feels the same way. So you need to identify and explain the different views that different people hold. The best answers, though, will add an extra ingredient. They will be aware that people sometimes have mixed feelings about things, perhaps they approve in some ways and disapprove in others, or perhaps their views change as circumstances change. These answers understand that people's ideas, beliefs and motives are complex, and cannot always be explained in straightforward terms. The following answer has all the necessary ingredients for full marks.

Supporters of the Nazis would generally have supported the SA. They would have regarded members of the SA with pride as people who were prepared to fight for their beliefs. Opponents of the Nazis would have felt just the opposite. They would have regarded the SA as vicious thugs who saw politics as an excuse to bully and threaten people. In fact, some Nazis probably regarded the SA with suspicion; they might have thought the violence was necessary but regrettable. As time went by, and particularly after the Nazis came to power, even strong supporters of the SA might have begun to change their minds. The SA continued to cause trouble and became a bit of an embarrassment, as Source C shows. Hitler certainly changed his mind because he had the leaders of the SA murdered, even though in 1926 he had wanted 'fanatical fighters'.

---

3 (a) Study Source A. Use your own knowledge to explain why the Nazis carried out 'racial examinations' of people in Germany. (7)

> **Examiner's tip** Source A shows a racial examination being carried out, but otherwise will not be of help in answering the question. Your task is to explain why the Nazis wanted such examinations to be done. Your answer must be based on an understanding of the Nazis' racial beliefs, such as their views on the superiority of the Aryan race, and their hatred of those races they believed to be inferior, such as the Jews. Remember that your answer should not be limited to a single reason or cause, and try to *explain* each of the reasons you give. So don't be satisfied by saying simply, 'The Nazis did these examinations because they wanted to find out who was Jewish.' This is true, and *identifies* a reason, but it does not explain why they would want to know who was Jewish and who was not. An answer which said, for example, that they wanted to know who was Jewish so that they could enforce their anti-Semitic (anti-Jewish) policies, such as preventing marriage between Aryans and Jews, would be *explaining* why such examinations were necessary. Any answer which can give a couple of such explanations would score a high mark. The following example was awarded the full seven marks.

Answers to Unit 5

Answer	Mark

The Nazis believed in racial theories which said that the pure Germans – the Aryans – were superior to all other races. Hitler was determined that other races would not be allowed to 'pollute' the Aryans, so it was vital to know who was Aryan and who was not. These examinations would demonstrate if someone was not Aryan and then they could be prevented from mixing with Aryans. For instance, Hitler passed the Nuremberg Laws against the Jews. If someone was identified as a Jew, they were not allowed to marry a German. This would make sure the German blood was 'pure'. Hitler hated the Jews more than any other race, and blamed them for all Germany's problems. He regarded them as enemies of the Nazi state. Examinations like the one in Source A would identify these enemies so they could be persecuted.

(b) Study Source B. Was Hitler's hatred of the Jews the main reason why they were persecuted in Nazi Germany? Use your own knowledge to explain your answer. (6)

> **Examiner's tip** This question asks you to consider the reasons why the Jews were persecuted in Nazi Germany, and to reach a judgement about which was the *most important* of these reasons. Clearly, Hitler hated the Jews and this was an important reason for their persecution in Nazi Germany. But were there other reasons for their persecution, and if so, were these reasons as important as Hitler's hatred or not? There is no single correct answer to questions like this. What is important is that you reach a conclusion, and support your conclusion using your knowledge of the period. The following answer claims that Hitler's hatred was *not* the most important reason, but this conclusion is based on a full consideration both of Hitler's policies and of an alternative reason, which is enough to gain full marks on this question. Source B fits in well with this argument because it provides evidence of anti-Semitism from the period *before* Hitler came to power.

From an early age Hitler had a hatred of the Jews, and when he came to power he encouraged their persecution. He believed they were an inferior race, and he blamed them for almost all of Germany's problems. He thought there was a world-wide Jewish conspiracy. Sometimes he claimed that the Jews would help the Communists take over the world, and sometimes he claimed that Jewish businessmen controlled all the world's business and industry for their own benefit. He was certainly responsible for the vicious persecution of the Jews in Nazi Germany such as the Nuremberg Laws, and later the Final Solution. However, it is difficult to be sure that he was the most important reason for this persecution. Anti-Semitism was common in Europe at that time. In Germany after the First World War many people blamed the Jews for Germany's defeat. You could say that one of the reasons why the Nazis gained popularity was because their racial views were approved of by many Germans. Source B shows that anti-Semitic propaganda was used before the Nazis came to power. We don't know whether Source B was a Nazi cartoon – it probably was – but they would not have used it if they did not think many people would agree with it. So Hitler when he came to power was doing what many people approved of. Many Germans were jealous of the Jews. When the Depression hit Germany the Jews were an obvious target to blame. Hitler could not have carried out his persecution of the Jews if many Germans had not already been anti-Jewish themselves. So the most important reason for the persecution of the Jews was the anti-Semitism of many German people. Hitler shared these views, but he did not create them.

Answers to Unit 5

Answer	Mark

(c) Study Source C. Not only Jews were persecuted in Nazi Germany. Use your own knowledge to explain why other groups of people were persecuted by the Nazis. (7)

> **Examiner's tip** Weaker answers will explain what it was about the Nazis that made them persecute people *in general*, rather than finding explanations for why they persecuted *particular* groups. For example, saying 'Different groups were persecuted in Nazi Germany because the Nazis were not prepared to tolerate any opposition' would not be a good answer to the question. It fails to identify groups that were persecuted, and to explain why the Nazis singled these particular groups out. You can use Source C to give you some ideas about groups of which the Nazis disapproved. But remember, a full explanation of why the Nazis persecuted some people does not just give reasons; it also explains why those reasons mattered. Make sure you know how to do this.
> Weak answers will just *identify* groups – 'The Nazis persecuted many other groups such as trade unionists.'
> Better answers will give a *reason* why those groups were persecuted – 'The Nazis persecuted trade unionists because Hitler did not want workers to have their own independent organisations.'
> The best answers will *explain the reasons* why those groups were persecuted – 'Hitler wanted to be able to control workers through a Nazi Party organisation, the Labour Front. He believed that free trade unions would prevent the Nazis controlling the workers. They might organise strikes, and oppose the Nazis, economic plans, so they had to be crushed.'
> There are lots of groups you could write about, such as Communists, trade unionists, gypsies, homosexuals and the insane. Your answer does not need to mention all of these. A full explanation, such as the example below, of why the Nazis persecuted a couple of these groups, would probably be enough for full marks.

The Nazis persecuted a lot of people. They did not tolerate opposition, so anyone who was against them would be persecuted. The Communists were a good example. Hitler believed there was a Communist plot to dominate the world, and that the Soviet Union was his greatest enemy. Anyone who was a Communist was, therefore, a threat because they would want to overthrow the Nazi state and replace it with a Communist one. But the Nazis also persecuted people who were not their opponents, just because of what they were. The Nazi racial theories said that certain races were inferior. This included the Jews, but also other groups such as gypsies. The Nazis wanted to make sure that the pure Aryan blood of the German people could not be 'polluted' by mixing with these other groups. At first they just persecuted these groups by taking away their rights, but later they tried to exterminate them in the Final Solution. Another group that suffered in this way were the mentally ill, who were abused because they did not fit in with Hitler's ideas of the 'master-race' being perfect in every way.

Answers to Unit 6

6 PAPER 2: SOURCES EXERCISE ON THE DEVELOPMENT STUDY

Answer	Mark

1 Study Sources A and B.
How far do these sources agree about the discovery and
development of penicillin? Explain your answer. (5)

> **Examiner's tip** One way of answering this question would be to identify all the agreements of detail between the two sources, e.g. they both say Fleming was studying the staphylococcus germ when he made the discovery, and they both say that he grew the mould. You could also explain that some parts of the story are described in one source but not in the other, e.g. the dishes being just above the level of the disinfectant in Source B. You would score reasonable marks by identifying these details but the top marks will go to answers which go beyond the details and examine the overall things these sources are suggesting about the discovery and the development of penicillin. The answer given below would score full marks because it shows how the sources agree on some things that they suggest, but disagree on others. It is also important to note the way that this answer is supported by details from the sources.

These sources agree that Fleming discovered penicillin by accident. They both show how he just happened to notice that the mould that had grown on the dirty plates was killing the germs. Source B even says that Fleming first said 'That's funny!', showing that he had noticed something he was not expecting. The sources seem to disagree about whether Fleming realised how useful penicillin could be. Source A says that he decided that it had no practical value in medicine but Source B says that he wrote articles about it and that he kept a supply of the mould. This means he knew it would be useful once someone had found a way of getting the pure penicillin out of the mould.

2 Study Source C.
How useful is this source as evidence about the discovery and development
of penicillin? Explain your answer. (5)

> **Examiner's tip** It is important that you use your knowledge and the details in the photograph to answer this question. An answer which says that Source A is useful because it is a photograph taken at the time when he made the discovery, or because it shows what his laboratory was like, will not get many marks. However, his laboratory does look untidy in the photograph and you can see all the dishes piled on top of each other. This matches up with the accounts in Sources A and B and shows how penicillin was discovered by accident.
> It is important to remember that the question asked 'How useful?' and so you must also try to explain a way in which this source is not useful. The answer below scores full marks by explaining both how the source is useful and how it is not so useful. It is useful as evidence about the discovery of penicillin, but it is not very useful as evidence about its later development.

67

Answers to Unit 6

Answer	Mark

The source is very useful because it shows you how untidy Fleming's laboratory was. You can see all the dishes he was using piled up. It was on a dish like this that completely by chance he found the mould and noticed it was killing the germs. The dishes in the photograph have obviously been left there some time and it would not be surprising that a mould had grown on one of them. The source is not very useful for telling you anything about the development of penicillin. People like Florey and Chain had to find a way of getting the pure penicillin from the mould and the photograph does not tell you anything about this.

---

3 Study Sources D and E.
   Does Source E support the claims made in Source D?
   Explain your answer. (6)

> **Examiner's tip** Source D tells us that Fleming gained all the glory for the discovery of penicillin. It goes on to explain that Florey was upset by this because he believed that Fleming deliberately claimed all the credit and glory for himself. Source E seems partly to support this claim and partly to show that it was wrong. It is important that you fully explain both of these points and that you support your answer with examples from the two sources. The answer which follows does all of this very well.

Source E does not really support the claims made in Source D. In Source D Florey complains about Fleming giving interviews and being photographed by the newspapers. He sees this as Fleming's way of getting all the glory for penicillin. But Source E shows that the reporters went to see Florey first and he refused to see them. They only went to Fleming after this. Florey can hardly blame Fleming when he himself had a chance to put his side of the story. Source E also shows that it wasn't Fleming who encouraged the publicity for St Mary's, but his head of department Sir Almoth Wright. In a way Source E also supports the claims in Source D. Florey complains that St Mary's took all the credit and Source E tells us that St Mary's needed publicity to help it raise money it badly needed. Sir Almoth Wright had used newspapers before to gain publicity for his hospital. So he probably claimed Fleming had done all the work on penicillin to get publicity for St Mary's.

---

4 Study Sources F and G.
   Which one of these two sources is the more reliable?
   Explain your answer. (7)

> **Examiner's tip** Few marks will be scored by concentrating on the type or date of the source, e.g. claiming that Source F is not reliable because it was published in a newspaper. It is important to (i) read what each source says, (ii) consider whether or not each source has a particular purpose, (iii) check what each source is saying against your knowledge of what happened or against other sources in the paper. Remember that the examiner is not so much interested in which source you decide is the more reliable as the reasons you give for your choice. It is also important to remember that you must evaluate both sources. Try and avoid making the common mistake of only writing about the source you have chosen as being the most reliable. There are several

Answers to Unit 6

Answer	Mark

> reasons for questioning the reliability of Source F. We know from Source E that Sir Almoth Wright wanted publicity for St Mary's. This might be the reason for him writing this letter. We also know from Source A that Fleming did not understand the importance penicillin might have in medicine. This disagrees with what Wright claims. There is also a good reason for doubting what Source G says, particularly when the tone of the source is examined as it is in the answer below. A careful reading of this answer will show that all the elements listed above as (i), (ii), (iii) are present. This answer would gain full marks.

I do not think Source F is very reliable. It is making great claims for Fleming but it has been written by Sir Almoth Wright who was Fleming's head of department. Source E says that Wright wanted publicity for St Mary's Hospital and so in Source F he is writing to The Times to claim all the credit for Fleming and St Mary's. Fleming was in his department and so it will also make Wright look good. For these reasons I do not think Source F is reliable. Wright also claims that Fleming knew penicillin would be important in medicine. But I know this was not the case. Fleming gave up on penicillin and it was Florey and Wright who realised how important it could be. At least Source G only claims that Fleming discovered penicillin which is right. It does not claim that he developed it. The trouble with Source G is that it is biased, as it describes Fleming as if he is a film star, e.g. 'dreamy blue eyes'. The author of Source G seems more interested in what he looked like than in him as a scientist. Despite this I think Source G is more reliable because it doesn't have Source F's reasons for exaggerating Fleming's importance.

---

5   Study Sources H, I and J.
    Do Sources I and J prove Source H to be wrong?   (7)

> **Examiner's tip**
>
> In Sources I and J Fleming appears to be arguing that he should not be given all the credit for penicillin. This clearly disagrees with the claims made in Source H by Florey that Fleming was taking all the credit. This does not necessarily mean that I and J prove Source H to be wrong. Can we trust Sources I and J? Is there other evidence in the paper that suggests that Fleming did take the credit, e.g. Sources E and F? Is there other evidence that Florey might be wrong?
> It is important that in answering this question you do not just use Sources H, I and J. The answer which follows starts off by making good use of these three sources but it then moves on to use other sources as well.

It looks as if Sources I and J do prove that Florey was wrong in Source H. He was arguing that Fleming was describing the development of penicillin in such a way as to get all the credit for himself. But in Source I Fleming is not doing this because he is saying that Florey did much of the important work. However, this does not mean that Fleming said this to everyone. Source I is a letter to Florey and Fleming is telling Florey that he deserves the credit. But Fleming might say one thing to Florey and then say the opposite to the newspapers. In fact this letter could be the letter that Florey talks about in Source H and it is clear the Fleming had not kept to his promise in the letter. Source J is much more important. This is a public speech and he is saying that

Answers to Unit 6

Answer   **Mark**

he did not realise how important penicillin was. This does seem to show that Florey's claims about Fleming were wrong. In Source J, Fleming is being honest. It is also the case that the other sources do not show Fleming as the one who was claiming all the credit. This was being done for him by his head of department, Sir Almoth Wright. So I do think that Source J shows that Source H is wrong.

6   **Study all the sources.**
      How far is the following statement supported by the sources in this paper?
      'Fleming deliberately grabbed the glory for the development of penicillin.'
      Use the sources and your knowledge to explain your answer.   **(10)**

> **Examiner's tip**   The final question in source papers usually requires you to use all the sources together to reach an overall conclusion. In fact, it is not necessary to use all the sources as long as you use most of them. What is far more important is what you do with the sources. Before you write your answer work out which sources support the statement and which oppose it. There will always be sources on both sides of the argument. Then try and explain how the first group of sources together support the statement. Using them together to construct an argument is much better than writing a separate paragraph on each source saying whether it does, or does not, support the statement. You can then explain how the other sources oppose the statement. Also remember that not all the sources can be trusted. Where this is the case make sure that you explain why there are some sources that you do not trust. Finally, you should try and reach an overall conclusion. The answer which follows does all of these things very well.

Most of the sources in this paper do not support the statement. Some of the sources show that it was not Fleming's fault that he got all the glory for penicillin. Sources E and F show that his head of department was really responsible for this. He wrote a letter to a newspaper claiming that Fleming should get the credit and we know that Wright was very good at getting publicity for his hospital. He had done it before and he did it about Fleming because he hoped to make more money for St Mary's. Source E also shows that Florey could have had the publicity if he had wanted but he turned it down. This is not Fleming's fault. Also Sources I and J shows that Fleming did not claim all the credit. He told scientists in America that he was not the one who realised the importance of penicillin.

However, some of the sources do appear to support the statement. Sources D and H say that Fleming claimed all the credit. But Source H is written by Florey. It is obvious that he was getting fed up with Fleming getting all the credit and he automatically blamed Fleming for this. I do not trust Source H for this reason. Florey probably did not realise that it was other people who were claiming the credit for Fleming. Overall, these sources show that it was not Fleming's fault.

Answers to mock examination paper

7 MOCK EXAMINATION PAPER

Answer	Mark

1 **Study Source A.**
According to this source were the contributions of Florence Nightingale and Mary Seacole similar or different? Explain your answer. (4)

Examiner's tip This question only carries four marks so you do not want to spend long on it. Try to avoid copying out passages from the source. The Examiner wants you to briefly summarise in your own words what this source tells you about Florence and Mary and point out ways in which their contributions were similar or different. Do not just describe what each of them did. You must explain how what they did was similar or different. Source A suggests that Florence's role was one of organising rather than looking after the soldiers herself. This contrasts with Mary who it seems worked directly with the troops. Even Florence's nurses, we are told, only did basic jobs and never left the wards. The answer which follows brings out the differences very clearly.

The contributions these two women made were very different. It sounds as if Mary Seacole got her hands dirty by going out onto the battlefield and looking after the soldiers there. Florence Nightingale was not actually involved in looking after patients herself – she left this to her nurses. She was in charge and so she organised everything. But even her nurses were not so involved as Mary Seacole. The source says that they only looked after soldiers who were in the hospitals. They did not go out on the battlefields like Mary.

2 **Study Sources B and C.**
These two descriptions of conditions in Scutari hospital are very different. Does this mean that one of them must be wrong? Explain your answer. (7)

Examiner's tip To simply claim that one of them must be wrong because they are so different will not get you many marks. Reasons for your answer must be given. There is no right answer to this question. The Examiner is looking for how well you support and explain your answer. You could argue that Hall is wrong because he was not interested in the welfare of the soldiers, and probably did not inspect the hospital very carefully, whereas Florence had to work there and would know the conditions much better. You could even argue that as the man in charge, Hall was trying to hide the dreadful conditions. On the other hand, Florence might be exaggerating the problems to increase her chances of receiving more supplies – remember she is writing to the British government. So they might both be wrong! On the other hand they might both be right. Florence's account was written after Hall's. This means that the fighting had been going on longer and the conditions may have grown worse. Or it might be that they interpreted the same conditions differently because of their backgrounds. Hall was an army man, he did not want his men to be pampered and so he would be satisfied with conditions that Florence, as a nurse, would not be satisfied with. All of these would be good answers. The important thing is that you use what you know about Florence and Hall to support your answer. The answer which follows does this well.

Answers to mock examination paper

Answer	Mark

I don't think that either of them is wrong. Hall inspected the hospital not long after the fighting started and things may not have been too bad then. Also he was a soldier and he did not want the men to be pampered. He didn't want the soldiers going soft through being pampered. So he was probably satisfied with the conditions and described them as he saw them. Florence Nightingale on the other hand was a nurse. She was interested in caring for the wounded soldiers. As a nurse she knew how important cleanliness was and so she was not satisfied with conditions that Hall would be satisfied with. Anyway conditions may have got worse by November because the fighting had been going on longer and there would be more wounded soldiers to look after in the hospital. So I don't think that either of them are lying. They are just describing things as they saw them.

3   Study Sources D and E.
     Which one of these two sources is more useful? Explain your answer.   (6)

> **Examiner's tip** The important question to ask yourself here is 'useful for what'. You must not, however, simply say this in your answer and move on to the next question. Both of these sources are useful, but they are useful in different ways. The important thing to do is to explain how each is useful and how each has its limitations. You should concentrate on the fact that one is a drawing from the time and one is a written account from much later. This means that they will convey different types of information. You should organise your answer around this fact. However, do not just claim that 'written accounts are better than drawings because they give you more information'. You must give examples of what you can learn from one source that you cannot learn from the other.
> For example, Source E is particularly useful because it tells you about what things were like before and after Florence started her work. Source D cannot do this because it is a drawing of one point in time. Source E also provides details of the type which cannot be provided by a drawing, e.g. the fall in the death rate – it tells you the benefits to the soldiers of Florence's work, which a drawing cannot do. On the other hand Source D shows you many details which Source E does not. The drawing gives you an impression of what the insides of the wards were like and it shows you e.g. how much space there was, how many beds were in each ward, the stove in the centre, the empty bed which shows it was not overcrowded.
> You can come to a conclusion at the end of your answer about which source you think is the more useful, but this must be after you have given examples of the advantages and disadvantages of each source. The answer which follows received full marks.

Source D is useful because it shows you what the hospital in Scutari actually looked like. You get a good impression of it in a way that a written description cannot give you. You can see that Florence Nightingale has made sure the ward is clean and tidy. There is plenty of space and the open windows provide fresh air. There is even one wounded soldier relaxing by the stove and one of the beds is empty which shows you that the hospital was not crowded. The whole place is calm and well organised. I think Source E is more useful because overall it tells you more. Source E tells you that before Florence Nightingale came the hospital was overcrowded and infested with rats. It then tells you how she improved conditions – by making it clean and by feeding the

Answers to mock examination paper

Answer	Mark

men properly. It also tells you that Florence's work led to the death rate falling from 40 per cent to 2 per cent. So Source E tells you how important Florence Nightingale's work was by comparing what it was like before and after her. The drawing cannot do this because it only shows you the hospital at one date.

4 Study Sources F and G.
How far do these two sources give similar impressions of Florence Nightingale and Mary Seacole? Explain your answer. (5)

> **Examiner's tip** It is important to support your answer with evidence from the two sources. First, read through Source F and try and form an impression of Florence Nightingale. Then do the same with Source G and Mary Seacole. You can then compare the impressions you have formed, which are probably quite different. When you write about these different impressions in your answer make sure you give supporting evidence as the answer below does.

I think these sources show that Florence Nightingale and Mary Seacole were very different. Florence seems to be more worried about moral matters than about looking after the patients. She did not think it right for women nurses to come into close contact with men patients. They were only allowed to do domestic chores and were not allowed into the wards after 8.30. If her nurses wanted to do more they had to leave and work somewhere else. Florence was so worried by these moral issues that she would rather have drunk men looking after the patients than her nurses. Mary Seacole on the other hand did not let anything get in the way of her caring for the wounded soldiers. Source G shows that her first concern was the soldiers. She was not worried by touching the soldiers and tried to comfort them even if this meant the soldiers holding her hand. She is a much more human, caring person. Florence does not seem all that interested in comforting the men, and takes more notice of the attitudes of society at this time.

5 Study Sources G and H.
Do you believe both of these sources? Explain your answer. (8)

> **Examiner's tip** The first thing to consider is that Source G is written by Mary herself. Can her account be trusted? It gives a very good impression of her as a wonderful caring person. It is also worth considering the title of her autobiography which might tell you something about the impression she is trying to convey about herself. On the other hand her account in Source G is supported by Source A. It does not matter whether you end up believing Mary or not, what is important is that you discuss these issues about her account. Both parts of Source H seem to raise fewer problems. They are both written by eye-witnesses. Both men must have been particularly impressed with her to have overcome the prejudices of the time about both women and about black people (most Jamaicans had been slaves earlier in the century), and it is significant that an army surgeon was ready to praise her. You can also use the Background Information to support what these two men are saying as the answer which follows does. You do score high marks for using other parts of the paper such as Source A and the Background Information where they are relevant to the question.

Answers to mock examination paper

Answer	Mark

I am not sure if I believe Source G. Mary could be writing this to give a good impression of herself. She is praising herself all the way through the source and the title of her autobiography seems to show that this is what she was trying to do. She might be doing this because of the resentment she feels about being turned down by Florence Nightingale and she feels that she has to prove herself. On the other hand her account is supported by Source A which tells about how she would walk through the battle-field looking for wounded soldiers to look after. I do believe Source H. These two men had no reason to lie about her. Indeed if anything they would be prejudiced against her. Many men at that time did not believe women should be doing this kind of work and it is surprising to find an army surgeon praising her. Also if you look at the Background Information you can see that the soldiers in Jamaica had also had a lot of respect for her as a doctor and so this supports Source H and makes it more believable.

6   Study all the sources. How far do these sources support the view that Florence Nightingale and Mary Seacole made important, but very different, contributions to the nursing of the soldiers in the Crimea? Make sure you use your own knowledge to interpret and evaluate the sources. (10)

> **Examiner's tip** Remember there are two things to consider here – (i) did they both make important contributions, and (ii) were their contributions different? The best way to answer this question is do a little planning in rough first. After reading the sources through it is clear that they did make very different types of contributions. Make a note of all the sources (including Background Information), that explain the importance of Florence's contribution, then make a note of all the sources that explain the importance of Mary Seacole's contribution. Use each set of sources to explain (i) how their work was important, and (ii) how their contributions were different. You do not have to use every single source (what use you make of the sources is more important than whether or not you have used every source), but you should try and use most of them. You also need to consider whether or not you can trust the sources you are using. It's no good using a source to support an argument if the source is unreliable. The answer which follows would be awarded very high marks.

These sources do support this statement. Sources A, C, D, and E all show that Florence Nightingale's work was very important. She made sure the hospital in Scutari was cleaned as Sources D and E show. More importantly she did all the organising. She made sure that everything the hospital needed was ordered and supplied like scrubbing brushes, food and operating tables. Source E shows this very clearly. Source A supports the view that she was mainly an organiser. Source E explains the importance of her work because she reduced the death rate from 40 per cent to 2 per cent. She was not perfect and perhaps she could have let some of the nurses do more than they did to help the wounded as Source F suggests but overall her work was very important. The only sources which might not be reliable are Sources A and C. Source A is written by someone who was more interested in Mary Seacole and might have underestimated the importance of Florence. In Source C Florence was trying to get more supplies and might have exaggerated the state of the hospital when she first got there. Sources A, G and H show how important Mary's work was. She did not organise things on a large scale and in that way was not as important as Florence but

74

Answer | Mark

she did care for individual soldiers. She went out of the hospital and cared for them on the battlefield. She cared for them herself and was very keen to bring them comfort as Source G clearly shows. Her contribution was different from Florence's. She did the nursing herself while Florence organised things. They were both important. Mary might have exaggerated what she did in Source G but Sources like H and A support the view that she did a lot of good and helped a lot of soldiers.

Acknowledgements

The authors and publishers gratefully acknowledge the following for permission to use questions and illustrations in this book:

Questions 3 (Unit 1); 1, 3 (Unit 2); 2 (Unit 3); 3 (Unit 4); and 1, 3 (Unit 5): Reproduced by kind permission of the Midland Examining Group. The Midland Examining Group bears no responsibility for the sample answers to questions taken from its past question papers which are contained in this publication. Questions 2 (Unit 1); 1 (Unit 3); 2 (Unit 4) and 2 (Unit 5): Reproduced by kind permission of the Northern Examinations and Assessment Board. The authors accept responsibility for the answers provided, which may not necessarily constitute the only possible solutions. Question 2 (Unit 2): Reproduced by kind permission of the Scottish Qualifications Authority (formerly SEB). Answers are the sole responsibility of the authors and have not been provided by the Board. Question 1 (Unit 4): Reproduced by kind permission of the Southern Examining Group. Any answers or hints on answers are the sole responsibility of the authors and have not been provided or approved by the Group. Question 1 (Unit 1): Reproduced by kind permission of London Examinations: A division of Edexcel Foundation (formerly ULEAC). Edexcel Foundation, London Examinations accepts no responsibility whatsoever for the accuracy or method of working in the answers given.

Print on p13, John Freeman; p14, Library of Riksuniversiteit, Utrecht; p15, © The British Museum; p17, TR Annan & Sons, Glasgow; prints on pp9, 19, and 36 reproduced by courtesy of Mansell/Time Inc./Katz; print on p31 reproduced by courtesy of Popperfoto; print on p25, Wiener Library, London. All reproduced with grateful thanks.